THE JOSSEY-BASS ACADEMIC ADMINISTRATOR'S GUIDE TO

Conflict Resolution

The Jossey-Bass Academic Administrator's Guides are designed to help new and experienced campus professionals when a promotion or move brings on new responsibilities, new tasks, and new situations. Each book focuses on a single topic, exploring its application to the higher education setting. These real-world guides provide advice about day-to-day responsibilities as well as an orientation to the organizational environment of campus administration. From department chairs to office staff supervisors, these concise resources will help college and university administrators understand and overcome obstacles to success.

We hope you will find this volume useful in your work. To that end, we welcome your reaction to this volume and to the series in general, including suggestions for future topics.

Other Jossey-Bass Academic Administrator's Guides:

Budgets and Financial Management by Margaret J. Barr
Meetings by Janis Fisher Chan
Hiring by Joseph G. Rosse and Robert A. Levin
Exemplary Leadership by James M. Kouzes and Barry Z. Posner

THE JOSSEY-BASS

ACADEMIC ADMINISTRATOR'S
GUIDE TO

Conflict Resolution

SANDRA I. CHELDELIN

ANN F. LUCAS

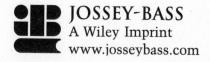

JOSSEY-BASS
A Wiley Imprint
www.josseybass.com

Published by Jossey-Bass
A Wiley Imprint
989 Market Street, San Francisco, CA 94103-1741   www.josseybass.com

Jossey-Bass books and products are available through most bookstores. To contact Jossey-Bass directly call our Customer Care Department within the U.S. at 800-956-7739, outside the U.S. at 317-572-3986 or fax 317-572-4002.

Jossey-Bass also publishes its books in a variety of electronic formats. Some content that appears in print may not be available in electronic books.

Library of Congress Cataloging-in-Publication Data

Cheldelin, Sandra.
   The Jossey-Bass academic administrator's guide to conflict resolution
/ Sandra I. Cheldelin, Ann F. Lucas.—1st ed.
      p. cm.
Includes bibliographical references and index.
   ISBN 0-7879-6053-5 (alk. paper)
   1. College personnel management—United States.   2. Conflict
management—United States.   I. Title: Academic administrator's guide to
conflict resolution.   II. Lucas, Ann F.   III. Title.
   LB2331.68.C54 2003
   378.1′94—dc22   2003018769

Printed in the United States of America
FIRST EDITION
PB Printing 10 9 8 7 6 5 4 3 2 1

CONTENTS

To our husbands:

R. Eugene Rice
and
Rawley D. Lucas

PREFACE

THE OFTEN USED metaphor of higher education as an ivory tower suggests that it is a tranquil place, far removed from the struggles of daily life and free of stress and conflict. But colleges and universities are made up of individuals who have been trained to be critical of others and of themselves, and socialized to probe arguments through analysis and to find flaws in the logic of others' thinking. With the exception of a few disciplines that aim to prepare graduates to work effectively with people, there are usually no courses on how to provide this criticism tactfully within a supportive relationship. There are no credits to be earned for learning to be a good team player or team leader.

PURPOSE

Within this conceptual framework, we have written a book on conflict resolution specifically for new leaders—or new in the role of leadership—employed in academic institutions. In the chapters that follow, we identify how conflicts can be diagnosed and what academic administrators can do to turn conflicts into problems to be solved. Learning about and using conflict management strategies can enhance one's professional development. Passively waiting for the combatants in an institutional setting to solve their own problems may take years, during which time others may become engaged in the conflict, sides are taken, coalitions are formed, and a department becomes fragmented. So knowing when and how to intervene in a conflict is important for leaders.

OVERVIEW OF THE BOOK

In Chapter One we lay the groundwork for understanding a conflict situation. We acknowledge that conflict can be both constructive and destructive, and we introduce conflict prevention, including how to work with change. A more detailed presentation of concrete ways in which academic administrators can analyze conflicts and begin to design interventions is the subject of Chapter Two. We offer a framework that considers conflict from the micro—psychological and social psychological—levels to the macro—cultural, traditional, and structural—levels of the university. These approaches can be generalized to a wide variety of conflicts.

In Chapter Three we explore sources of conflict within the individual. Although the term *conflict* is usually thought of in terms of two or more parties, intrapersonal conflict can be a significant cause of problems. This is particularly true when negative thinking, and making assumptions about another's motivation, sets the framework for the way we form a concept or a perception. We present strategies for changing irrational and negative thinking to positive rational thought. Stress also makes it difficult to view a situation or a person objectively, especially when that person annoys us. We discuss three of the major stresses in an academic leader's life: role conflict, role ambiguity, and role overload.

The most common conflict academic administrators have to cope with is interpersonal conflict between two individuals,—usually within their departments. Chapter Four covers conflict between two people that may be a temporary flare-up or what seems like intractable long-term resentments between two individuals who work together. Being aware of the causes of conflict, the predictable stages of conflict, and four of the possible outcomes of conflict can make us appreciate that maintaining a good relationship is just as important as simply resolving the conflict. Identifying a conflict and reframing it so that it becomes a problem to be solved instead of a cause for dysfunctional behavior are important skills for an administrator to cultivate.

An understanding of the major approaches for managing conflict, and when they work and when they don't, provides an array of choices for academic administrators who must deal with conflict to keep it from disrupting a department. Chapter Five provides strategies for preventing and solving specific problems, including how to deal effectively with curmudgeons, and offers administrators effective approaches for untangling serious conflicts. It also includes important information about group formation and effective group functioning.

More complex conflicts in the academy show up between departments. Intergroup conflicts are discussed in Chapter Six. There are classic stories about the academic program versus the athletic program; perks and salary discrepancies between administrators and staff; the expense of grounds and buildings upkeep versus attention to updating classrooms. Managing shared revenues, juggling course assignments, allocating space, organizing the time slots for courses, and maintaining management and staff relationships are all examples of potential interdepartmental strife. We discuss intergroup competition and the social influences that increase group conformity and compliance.

Informal and well-used third party interventions such as negotiation, facilitation, mediation, and arbitration are introduced in Chapter Seven, along with a framework for matching conflict analysis with the most effective intervention. It is also important to know when conflict can and cannot be resolved by the administrator. Sometimes the legal department, human resources, ombuds officers, or counseling services staff should become involved.

Finally, two cases are included in Chapter Eight that deal with collaborating with other departments. The second case provides a model for managing conflict and gives you an opportunity to practice your skills in diagnosing and designing interventions to handle conflict.

AUDIENCE

This book is written for new academic administrators of colleges and universities—or veteran members of the academy who are now new in their roles as academic administrators—as a personal guide for developing knowledge and skills in handling conflict. Nevertheless, it can also be used by directors of departments or anyone aspiring to become an academic leader or chair of a committee, particularly across sectors of the academy.

Graduate students interested in academic administration and human resources development will find this book a window into the challenges and opportunities when leading a department or unit. The book is designed to help sharpen conflict management skills. Even faculty who want to increase their understanding of managing conflict in the classroom, or online, will find valuable ideas to increase their leadership potential and model effective conflict management techniques for their students.

In consulting with departments in a large number of colleges and universities, we have uncovered compelling evidence that dysfunctional departments exist in research and comprehensive universities, liberal arts colleges, professional schools, and community colleges. They lack agreed-upon methods for managing conflict that often result in conflict being swept under the rug. Practical strategies for dealing with a variety of conflicts found in our colleges and universities are discussed throughout the book. We have intentionally limited references in the text but have included a list of helpful resources at the end for further study.

ACKNOWLEDGMENTS

To the many thousands of administrators, including managers, supervisors, chairs, deans, faculty and administrative leaders, and boards of directors, from around the country and abroad, with whom we have worked and who have willingly shared their experiences with us, we thank you. We have presented some of your struggles hoping we can collectively learn from them to prevent or contain our own.

This book has been a genuine collaborative project and for that reason the authorship is listed alphabetically. Although we each took primary responsibilities for first drafts of chapters, we offered each other our insights, feedback, criticism, and support. We know firsthand the benefits of working collaboratively. We hope you, too, will benefit from this and enjoy what is to come.

Sandra I. Cheldelin
Ann F. Lucas

ABOUT THE AUTHORS

SANDRA CHELDELIN is associate professor of conflict analysis and resolution and former director at the Institute for Conflict Analysis and Resolution (ICAR) at George Mason University, Fairfax, Virginia. She has served on the faculty and as provost at the McGregor School of Antioch University in Yellow Springs, Ohio, and on the faculty and as academic dean at the California School of Professional Psychology in Berkeley. Prior to those positions she was on the faculty and was director of Education, Development, and Resources at the medical school at Ohio University and instructor in the Behavioral Sciences Department at Columbus State College.

Throughout her career of more than thirty years in the academy she has been an active practitioner. As a psychologist and expert in organizational behavior, she has applied her skills to support collaborative leadership, mediation, conflict resolution, strategic planning, and institution building to more than one hundred organizations including colleges and universities, medical schools, associations, treatment facilities, religious organizations, and corporations, both domestically and abroad.

Sandra has served as keynote speaker and invited lecturer on workplace issues including conflict resolution, change, and violence. She is co-editor of the textbook *Conflict: From Analysis to Intervention.* She is the author and coauthor of a number of articles and chapters. She has served on the Executive and Core Committees of the Professional and

Organizational Development Network in Higher Education and on the Board of Directors of the National Communities of Peacemaking and Conflict Resolution (NCPCR), the Northern Virginia Mediation Services (NVMS), CRInfo, and the Glen Helen Association (an environmentalist group).

Sandra earned her B.S. degree in sociology at Oregon State University and both her M.Ed. and Ed.D. degrees in psychological foundations of education at the University of Florida. She is a member of the American Association for Higher Education and the American Psychological Association.

ANN F. LUCAS is professor of organizational development and former campus chair in the Department of Management at Fairleigh Dickinson University (FDU), where she is founder and former director of the Office of Professional and Organizational Development. She has also been a full-time faculty member in the doctoral program in clinical psychology and has served as chair of the Psychology Department at FDU. She has also had a part-time practice in clinical psychology for more than twenty-five years and consulted with more than thirty Fortune 500 companies, hospitals, and federal and city government agencies.

A consultant in leadership in higher education on the international level as well as in this country, Ann has conducted workshops for more than 7,000 chairs and deans on more than 175 college and university campuses on the U.S. mainland and in Hawaii, Australia, New Zealand, Canada, Italy, and Puerto Rico. She has also been a presenter at over 125 professional and disciplinary conferences.

A licensed psychologist with a diplomate from the American Board of Professional Psychology, and a fellow in the Academy of Clinical Psychology, Ann Lucas received her B.S. degree in psychology from Seton Hall University and her M.A. and Ph.D. degrees in psychology from Fordham University, Rose Hill Campus. Her more than forty publications include four books, chapters in books, and articles in the area of leadership in the academic department, team building, the chair's role in enhancing teaching effectiveness, increasing faculty scholarly productivity, motivating students, performance evaluation, conflict resolution, outplacement in a university setting, and faculty development. Her most recent book, *Leading Academic Change: Essential Roles for Department Chairs,* was published by Jossey-Bass in 2000.

Nominated by her department chair and supported by faculty members in the department, Dr. Lucas was selected for the award of Outstanding Educators of America. She has also been the recipient of the Zucker Memorial Award for outstanding teaching and dedication to higher education by the students in her college of the university. Dr. Lucas is the recipient of the William E. Cashin Distinguished Service Award for Outstanding Contributions to the Academic Chairpersons Conference and the Study of Academic Administration (1999).

THE JOSSEY-BASS ACADEMIC ADMINISTRATOR'S GUIDE TO

Conflict Resolution

1

Understanding Conflict

WELCOME TO OUR STUDY about conflict resolution in higher education. We begin this chapter by laying the groundwork for understanding a conflict situation. After all, to understand its resolution, we must first know what conflict is. We will introduce important concepts and illustrate how to use them. We discuss how conflict is often destructive—even though it need not be so—and how conflict can be changed into a constructive interaction. We conclude with a discussion of conflict prevention—the easiest way to handle conflict.

CONFLICT DEFINED

In the field of conflict resolution, there are many definitions of conflict. One that we think is both basic and applicable to most conflicts in higher education comes from William Wilmot and Joyce Hocker in their study of interpersonal conflict. They identify three conditions: (1) some kind of expressed struggle between at least two parties, (2) these parties have an interdependent relationship, and (3) these parties perceive they are getting interference from each other in achieving their goals. Using this definition to think about conflict is helpful because it implies that conflicts will not change until there is a change in the parties' *perceptions* about the other(s) and a change in their behavior.

Let's imagine that Charlie, a student at your college, needs to drop a course in the third week of the semester because of an imposed change in his work schedule. The university policy says that at this point students must pay 40 percent of the tuition. Yet Charlie believes he has a special case and therefore should not be assessed the fee. After all, it is not his fault that he can no longer attend the class. Is this a conflict? Not yet, though it has all the ingredients to become one. Conflict will occur when Charlie is told by Eileen, the enrollment management supervisor—to whom Charlie later appeals—that he must still pay 40 percent of the tuition when he drops the class. Now there are incompatible goals (Charlie's special case versus Eileen's responsibility to consistently apply university rules). Charlie perceives interference from Eileen when she makes him pay. What would you do? Can you prevent this from becoming a conflict?

Conflict cannot occur unless there is an interaction between the parties, and therefore the responses Charlie and Eileen have toward each other are critical. (Chapter Four discusses individual preferences or styles of handling this interaction such as taking an aggressive position or avoiding it to prevent confrontation.) As Charlie and Eileen perceive interference from each other, the interaction is likely to escalate to a conflict situation. If they believe they can work together to find a solution, they are likely to respond in ways that prevent a conflict.

WORKING WITH CONFLICT

As adults, most of us have considerable experience with conflict and have learned ways of coping with it. We have encountered conflict since early childhood. In our families we struggled with siblings and parents and learned, early on, ways to handle others and get our way or lose the struggle. Over the years we developed *preferences* for dealing with conflict. Some of us remain quiet, calm, and restrained; others blow up; some prefer to fight behind the scenes; many avoid or ignore it; and a few intentionally try to get issues out on the table for discussion. During our years in school we struggled with peers and teachers and learned strategies to get ahead, to compromise, to work collaboratively, to be aggressive, or to give in. In the workplace we have struggled with coworkers, bosses, and subordinates and learned how to work with issues of power, authority, and control. In the news we are bombarded with stories of terrorism, war, and political in-fighting, and we continue to learn about protracted, enduring conflicts that seem nearly impossible to resolve. We are savvy about who to fear and who to bully. We are cognizant about issues of status, class, litigation, and fairness. And we bring this rich mosaic of experience-based information about conflict to our work in the university. So why is it, then—with everything that we have all learned—that conflict continues to persist in the academy?

Let us first consider the nature of the organizational context. American higher education is special in its structure, mission, and governance. One way that it is special is its decentralized model—public and private, four-year and two-year, proprietary and nonprofit. Colleges and universities establish their own decision-making models—embedded in and consistent with the larger culture of similar institutions that are public, private, four-year, two-year, and so on. Another variable to consider is that higher education is one of the few places where inconvenient questions can be asked, multiple voices can be heard, and various perspectives can be considered. This means that the heterogeneity of the people, ideas, and issues will encourage differences and therefore increase the likelihood of conflict. The academy also has a primary leadership role because it provides the intellectual and moral foundation for our youth to become leaders and members of society. Yet the rapid advance of knowledge in many fields of study makes this particular task daunting. In addition to higher education's organizational uniqueness and complexity, its context is embedded in a time of challenging resource limitations and enormous economic pressures, where authority and governance structures continue to be scrutinized, and external accountability is increasingly called forth.

WHEN CONFLICT IS DESTRUCTIVE

Returning to and based on our personal experiences, it is not uncommon when we hear the word *conflict* to think of concepts such as war, anger, destruction, terror, hostility, anxiety, alienation, and frustration. Particularly in U.S. culture, conflict is generally perceived as negative. Simple misunderstandings or minor disagreements can shift into full-fledged battles and become quite destructive. How does this happen? We know that there are three common conditions that encourage conflict escalation: when the parties *perceive* competition over scarce resources, *perceive* the use of threatening and contentious influence patterns (bullying, shoving, challenging, posturing, and so on), and *perceive* unfair highlighting of specific personal characteristics of others (gender, race, disability, and so on). Any of these three conditions will likely result in escalation; the presence of more than one will make conflicts even more difficult to manage or resolve.

Competition over Scarce Resources

The 1990s were financially good for higher education. The economy was unusually strong, investments yielded high returns, and alumni were willing to increase giving. Administrators were adding programs and staff, and upgrading technology. Recently, though, there has been a sharp change in available resources. We read about mandated cuts in budgets across the country. The financing of new buildings is disappearing. At best, the era of growth and prosperity has been put on hold. Why is this important? Because not only do we *perceive* limited resources, there actually *are* limited resources, and a common response to this situation is acting on the belief that we must find ways to "fight" for our share or we will lose. When this happens it is difficult to find much evidence of collaborative teamwork because managers hold their cards closer to their chests and withhold information they think might be dangerous to disclose. If people believe that the biggest bully will get the largest return, what happens? Conflict escalates and finger pointing about the "other" becomes more prevalent.

Threatening Influence Patterns

When leaders and managers experience limited resources, competition between units erupts. This is often accompanied by overt accusations. When the president or provost announces a university-wide multimillion dollar budget cut that will affect all units, posturing between department heads is predictable. Department heads argue—in newspapers or at meetings or administrative forums—that some departments such as athletics should have greater cuts than other departments such as recruitment or that revenue-generating academic programs should get special dispensation over revenue-spending departments such as technology support. In other words, one department or unit makes a case for fewer cuts at the expense of another department or unit. The other group, of course, experiences this as threatening. Coalitions emerge, one against another.

Long-term, simmering, and unresolved conflicts present themselves over and over again during difficult times. A classic example on many of our campuses is the unresolved conflicts between administrators and faculty that result in the two groups periodically threatening each other. Threatening influence patterns are not limited to large groups across departments, however. It is very common to find evidence of threat and escalated conflict within departments and between individuals.

Leaders and managers must use their position power very carefully to keep employees, members of departments, or other subordinates from feeling abused. Active listening and demonstrating empathy and concern about specific situations is always helpful. Returning to the case of Charlie and Eileen, if she expresses sympathy for his position but can turn to an objective source—the catalogue—which states that students must pay 40 percent of the tuition, Charlie is not so likely to feel that she is using her power at his expense. How Eileen and Charlie handle themselves is important. Their behavior can escalate the conflict situation or help them come to an understanding that seems fair, even if one of the parties does not particularly like the outcome.

Attacks on Personal Characteristics

Minor conflicts escalate quickly when there are inappropriate accusations related to such personal characteristics as race, gender, class, sexual preference, and so on. Talking unfavorably about others based on their role—"administrator," "staff," or "student"—also results in similar reactions. We don't like to be categorized, and we certainly don't like it when a categorization is delivered or meant in a derogatory way. Joe, a long-time employee of a graphics and design department, has a history of telling off-color jokes. Libby, the new employee, heard a series of his jokes, often at the expense of women, and took offense. She discussed her concerns with another female colleague and learned that many in the department were unwilling to challenge him. They mostly dismissed his behavior by such comments as "Oh, that's just Joe. He does that all the time to every group. No one is untouched." Unsatisfied, Libby decided to challenge Joe about his offensive joke telling. Joe got defensive and responded with anger: "Maybe these jokes have way too much truth to them. You are certainly making me see that!" She was furious that he was so insensitive. Their conflict escalated quickly when he accused her of lacking a sense of humor and being "boringly straight."

The Impact of Escalation

Group process and group cohesiveness become significantly impaired when simple conflicts turn destructive and escalate. The following are common results:

- Good feelings are undermined
- Cohesiveness is fractured
- Positions are polarized
- Difficulty in seeking cooperation is created
- Differing values emerge
- Comments are later regretted

The escalation of the conflict between Libby and Joe met all of these criteria. First, it undermined good feelings. Libby felt she was being devalued as a woman and as a result was unwilling to make any special efforts to respond to Joe as a colleague. The exchange also fractured potential cohesiveness within the department because colleagues began to take sides. Polarization of positions emerged and justified each party's behavior toward the other: "Why did we hire her in the first place?" and "How can he get away with such archaic ways of working with colleagues? The academy is no longer an 'old boys' network!" Once positions become polarized, it is difficult to see any common ground or seek cooperation. This would violate "face-saving" and be perceived as caving into the other's position. The differences in values become clear and accusations are espoused— "he is such a sexist" and "she is such a prude." Often disputants make comments to and about each other that are later regretted.

We have all experienced conflicts with destructive outcomes. Yet this need not be the case. How we respond to conflict escalation depends upon our ability to listen carefully and consider options. When we are locked into positions and develop scripts about another person, it is difficult to change our perceptions. One way to break the logjam is to ask: "How can conflicts—this one in particular—be helpful in any way?"

WHEN CONFLICT IS CONSTRUCTIVE

There are many examples where conflict turns out to be constructive for individuals and groups. First, constructive conflicts encourage open discussion and allow full exploration of each party's needs, concerns, values, and interests—the essential ingredients of authentic communication. Second, conflict is constructive if it provides an opportunity to release pent-up emotions. Griping and complaining often help people let off steam so that they can move on. Making space for complaints—formal and informal meetings, time on agendas, hallway conversations—encourages colleagues to take the risk of voicing their concerns. Third, if solutions to problems emerge in the open discussion or griping sessions, these solutions are likely to have greater buy-in. Paradoxically, conflict can build cohesiveness as people begin to have a history together of "surviving" conflict. They are able to solve other problems and negotiate other changes that are likely to occur.

Constructive conflict provides an excellent opportunity to demonstrate that even when colleagues make mistakes, or deliver remarks they later regret, or perceive another person as being inappropriate, these concerns and errors can be revisited and repaired. As differences arise, new solutions can be generated with appropriate support and willingness to understand one another.

An actual case illustrates one way conflict can be constructive. Jim and Diane were two members of an important task force. They were constantly fighting about what each believed should be the direction of the committee's work. After three difficult meetings, Susan, a third task force member, told the group that she did not want to serve on the task force if Jim and Diane's bickering continued. She suggested that each meeting's agenda include designated times for full discussion on controversial topics. Once everyone had an opportunity to present her or his perspective, the group would support the greatest consensus. This small intervention worked and allowed all voices to be heard and considered. It made a special place for discussing real differences, and a process was put into place to move ahead. The task force significantly increased its productivity and got its work completed.

PREDICTING AND PREVENTING CONFLICT

Throughout the book we will be talking about how to analyze conflict situations and strategies to manage or resolve them. Some situations, however, are predictable precursors for conflicts. Two common precursors in our colleges and universities are initiating any significant *change*—welcomed or not—and being involved in any individual or group *transition* process. These are not necessarily sufficient causes of conflict, but under these conditions academic administrators should be on the alert for early detection and possible prevention of conflict.

We are all currently experiencing many changes. A large population bubble is aging. Senior administrators and faculty will be retiring in increasing numbers. As key university citizens, they will need to be replaced. Early-career administrators and faculty already reflect differences in gender, ethnicity, backgrounds, and values. These differences will only be exaggerated over the next decade. We are also shifting the focus in the teaching and learning process away from faculty, and how much they know, toward students, and how best they learn. The massive influx of technology, the creation of virtual universities, the dramatic increases of online courses, the shifts from books and periodicals to web and electronic databases, and the availability of "smart classrooms" for teaching—wired rooms with the best technology readily available, including computer terminals at every seat and multimedia capabilities for faculty, organized in pods for student learning communities—all impact the roles and tasks of staff as well as faculty and students. Administrators are clearly playing a more direct role in the academic enterprise than in previous decades.

As the economy shifts, so does competition between and among colleges, universities, and corporate classrooms. There are increased demand for accountability at all levels and increased attention to measurable outcomes. As if this isn't hard enough, we also find those outside the academy no longer give us the reverence or prestige we once enjoyed. In fact, there is growing evidence of contempt for such perks as tenure and nine-month contracts, especially in times of economic uncertainty. Finally, nearly all of us know what happens when a college or university has new leadership, either at the top with the president or with heads of departments. These leaders enthusiastically initiate change: they want to make their mark; they want to change the ratings with *U.S. News and World Report;* they want to change their Carnegie Classification from a comprehensive to a research university. The list goes on.

When Change Is Conflictual

Change is seldom embraced with full welcome. We get comfortable with our patterns of doing business, and change introduces dissonance. The dissonance can quickly escalate to conflict, even though the change that caused it may begin with the best of intentions. This is well illustrated by the following case. Mary became the ninth member of an administrative support office for public relations and outreach. The department members were particularly pleased because they had successfully recruited her to join their all-male group of eight. They knew they needed more women in the department, and this was a beginning and important step. They scheduled a two-day retreat shortly after Mary joined them, both to celebrate and welcome her, and to include her in the planning process of their next couple of years' activities. The retreat was held at the second home of a member of the department, fifty miles from the university, on the edge of a golf course. The morning and evening of the first day were work-related sessions while the afternoon was time-out for play. All eight men in the department were golfers, played together regularly, and had prescheduled tee-off times for two sets of four, back-to-back. That left Mary—also a golfer, albeit not a very good one, but no one asked—to "go shopping, or read, or relax by the pool" or whatever she wanted during the four-hour break. Though the men appeared oblivious to any real problem, Mary was deeply offended. Within a very short period of time, she threatened to break her contract and leave the university.

Most new employees arrive with optimism and hope that they have made the right decision. Mary was no exception. Yet the conflict escalated quickly and became destructive because it met several of the conditions we outlined earlier. This simple incident undermined good feelings. When the men left to play golf, Mary felt intentionally but undeservedly excluded and perceived it would be difficult to have a full voice in the department. A fracture in the cohesiveness of the department resulted. Prior to Mary's hire, all members of the department worked (and played) well together. Now polarization of positions emerged to justify the men's behavior of playing golf. Even colleagues outside the department took sides, and coalitions formed. The issue of gender became dominant in the department, and colleagues, out of frustration and high emotion, said things they later regretted.

How could all of this have been prevented? The men's good intentions of hiring a woman could have been successful had they anticipated ways they would need to change to accommodate a new female member of the department. Mary could have anticipated that gender problems would likely occur when entering an all-male department and could have been prepared to help them. Someone in the department—an informal peacemaker—could bring the group together to initiate an apology, especially for the unintended consequences of the retreat.

Responses to Change and Transition

Research on change informs us that regardless of good or bad intentions, we have fairly predictable responses to it. We know change always generates stress, which is often translated into resistance. Even planned change will meet resistance. Some of our understanding about responses to change is informed by the distinctions made by William Bridges more than two decades ago in his work on transitions. He says that most of our resistance is not so much to the change itself, but to the transition involved in the change: the transition from old leadership to new leadership; from an all-male department to a mixed-gender department; from a faculty that is predominately white, male, and over sixty to a faculty of women, people of color, and twenty or more years younger. Change occurs when something new starts or something old stops, and it occurs at a particular point in time. But transitions cannot be localized in time that way. There is a gradual psychological process of reorientation. Change is situational and starts with a new beginning while transitions are psychological and start with an ending. Transition means letting go of our old attitudes, behaviors, or ways we conducted business.

Many of the changes we experience in higher education can best be understood by their transitional nature. Why is this important? Understanding change as transition is a useful framework to prevent a situation of change from escalating into full-fledged conflict, as it did in the case of Mary and her all-male department. Academic administrators should take seriously the stages of transitions: letting go of the old (ending), taking time to sort out what the group wants to do, and then starting with the new (beginning). What we typically do, instead, is start something new (beginning) before we stop doing what we did (ending). This often results in resistance and then moves to conflict. The department hired Mary (new) without fully considering the impact it would have on how they conducted business (old).

SUMMARY

When there is an expressed struggle between at least two parties who have an interdependent relationship and perceive they are getting interference from one another, conflict is likely to emerge. Conflict can be useful in a department, but often it is not. We know that the transitional nature of change is also a precursor to conflict and that the academy is currently fraught with change, from both internal and external pressures: the massive influx of technology, the development of virtual universities, the changing nature of the faculty and student bodies, the legislatures' and trustees' challenges to lifetime employment and tenure, organizational restructuring, downsizing, and shifting finance structures are just a few examples.

In the chapters that follow, we will look at frameworks for analyzing conflicts and identify ways you as a new academic administrator can understand when you are in the middle of a conflict, and what you can do about it. In addition, we will encourage you to be vigilant in seeking ways to contain the necessary conditions for conflict to erupt. Help members of your group find ways to work and learn together. Explore the ways your differences are both helpful and hard for one another. Collaborative projects, opportunities for small and large group problem solving, and including agenda items at meetings specifically requesting areas of concern are all techniques of prevention. As you become a student of conflict management and resolution, you will come to appreciate the importance of conflict analysis. In Chapter Two we present a framework for a conflict analysis process. Nevertheless, any opportunity to prevent full-fledged conflict is well worth exploring.

2

A Framework for Conflict Analysis

CHAPTER ONE LAID THE groundwork for understanding a conflict situation, explaining its constructive and destructive characteristics. We also introduced conflict prevention. We turn now to a deeper analysis and understanding of the dynamics of a conflict and offer a framework to help you explore conflict situations. We conclude by introducing strategies for intervention, which are more fully developed in Chapter Seven.

Just as there are several definitions of conflict, there too are several frameworks for analyzing conflict. We offer one that is both easy to use and thorough. Figure 2.1, A Framework for Conflict Analysis, is adapted from the work of Sandra Cheldelin and her two colleagues Daniel Druckman and Larissa Fast at the Institute for Conflict Analysis and Resolution. The simple framework considers three nested concentric circles that represent three levels of analysis.

At the framework's inner circle or core we consider the micro, psychological aspects of the conflict: the *type* of conflict, its *sources,* and its *dynamics.* The middle circle focuses on the contextual issues, including the identities of the parties in conflict and the situations that impact their conflict. Finally, the outer circle forces us to consider the macro or *structural* aspects of the conflict including the *traditions* and *culture* of our institutions. We offer corresponding questions for each level to guide your analysis. Once you have a fairly accurate understanding of the problem,

Figure 2.1. A Framework for Conflict Analysis

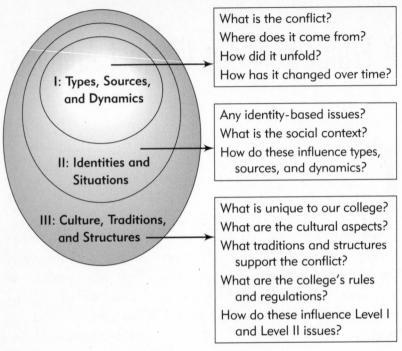

What is the conflict?
Where does it come from?
How did it unfold?
How has it changed over time?

Any identity-based issues?
What is the social context?
How do these influence types, sources, and dynamics?

What is unique to our college?
What are the cultural aspects?
What traditions and structures support the conflict?
What are the college's rules and regulations?
How do these influence Level I and Level II issues?

I: Types, Sources, and Dynamics

II: Identities and Situations

III: Culture, Traditions, and Structures

Source: Adapted from Cheldelin, Druckman, and Fast (2003).

you can then, and should only then, design an appropriate intervention strategy (as discussed in Chapter Seven).

LEVEL I ANALYSIS OF MICRO ISSUES: TYPES, SOURCES, AND DYNAMICS

Analysis of any conflict begins by considering the issues reflected in the inner core circle: the types, sources, and dynamics of the conflict. We seek answers to such questions as:

- What is the conflict?

- Where does it come from?

- How did it unfold?

- How has it changed over time?

- What has been the result?

By organizing these questions in terms of types, sources, and dynamics, we gain a greater understanding of the social and psychological dimensions of the conflict situation.

Types of Conflict

The parties' motivations and behavior—their *issues, hopes, orientation toward conflict,* and *levels of interaction*—are the ingredients of conflict types. To articulate the issues and underlying desires requires us to be diligent inquirers and careful listeners. What questions can we ask the parties to help us understand their issues? How can we provide opportunities for them to tell their stories, showing us how they frame their concerns, and what they want as outcomes?

A simple way of considering the parties' orientations toward conflict is to look at their view of the rights, values, and concerns of individuals on both sides of the conflict. Conflict orientations as developed by Kenneth Thomas and Ralph Kilmann are more fully explored in Chapter Five. Briefly, an inability to confront a disagreement, and thus ignore one's own rights as well as the rights of others, leads to *avoidance* as a preference—to not deal with the conflict. Where there is a low regard for one's own rights and needs and a high concern for the other's, the preference is to *accommodate* or give in to what the other party wants. A high regard for one's own rights and a low regard for the other's indicate a strong possibility that *aggressive* or forcing tactics will be used. Many conflicts are resolved by *compromise,* whereby both parties have some of their rights and needs met, but not all. Finally, some prefer to find ways in which both parties' rights and needs are fully addressed. This requires an ability to *collaborate.* Ask yourself these questions: What appear to be the two parties' preferences—avoidance, accommodation, aggression, compromise, collaboration—for dealing with this conflict? How do these preferences present themselves in this conflict?

We also consider the placement of the conflict interaction using traditional *levels:* intra-individual, interpersonal, intragroup, and intergroup domains. These are more fully explained in Chapters Three, Four, Five, and Six. Where is the locus of this conflict? Is the problem that an individual is not coping well with her or his own issues and concerns? Is it primarily between two people? Is it between members of your own department? Does the conflict present itself between groups such as your department and another department? Fully understanding the conflict situation, including the level of conflict interaction, ultimately helps you select the appropriate intervention to use.

Sources of Conflict

Diagnosing a conflict also requires us to consider the conflict sources: the parties' *relationships, needs, interests, values,* and *ideologies* that can serve as constraints to effective communication and collaborative teamwork. Few conflicts have a single source; the most protracted and enduring conflicts nearly always have multiple sources. When the primary source of the conflict is *relationship*-based the parties demonstrate tension, lack of trust, hostility, anger, frustration, and resentment toward each other. Effective and collaborative teamwork is especially difficult. When people have differing *needs* and *interests,* these differences become the driving forces in the conflict. When *values* vary, the parties operate from contradictory assumptions about the world, and often these different ideological positions make conflict resolution more difficult. Again, by sorting out the sources, you are in a better position to design an appropriate strategy for intervention.

Dynamics of Conflict

When there are real and significant differences in *interests, power, perceived injustices,* and *needs,* the situation is ripe for conflict to erupt. It is the dynamics—the interaction of these perceived differences and injustices—that escalate predisposing conditions to actual conflicts. A colleague, Tamra d'Estree, illustrates these dynamics with an Alka Seltzer demonstration. With a glass of water in one hand and the white tablet in the other, she simply drops the tablet in the water, thus beginning a new process. At first a few bubbles form. Soon thereafter the water is foaming, and a dramatic chemical reaction unfolds. Like most conflicts, this unfolding entity nicely demonstrates what happens as conflicts escalate: they appear to take on a life of their own. Similarly, when *interests, values,* or *needs* are not being met—what the parties think is desirable for them—and when there is an imbalance of *power* and *perceived injustice,* conflict is predictable.

We know that significant socioeconomic differences such as large discrepancies in salary, job status, and title—for example, faculty versus clerical or maintenance staff—encourage class-based conflicts. Significant political and ethnic differences encourage identity-based conflicts. Similarly, significant cultural differences encourage worldview-based conflicts. These are the backdrop of our conflict analysis at Levels II and III, expanding the social psychological components of the conflict (Level I) to include contextual and structural issues.

LEVEL II ANALYSIS OF MESO ISSUES: IDENTITIES AND SITUATIONS

Returning to Figure 2.1, the second level of analysis considers contextual issues: the setting within which the conflict occurs that helps frame the conflict. Two contextual issues are especially important at this level: identity and situation. We explore such questions as:

- What are the *identity* concerns of the parties?

- How does the way they think about themselves influence the conflict?

- What is the *situation* in which they are in conflict?

- What is the social context of the conflict?

- In what ways are these second-level issues—identities and situations—influencing the first-level components—types, sources, and dynamics—of the conflict?

Identity

Identity is at the heart of people's sense of themselves: how they define themselves, how they relate to and make order of their environment, and ultimately, how they feel safe both physically and psychologically in the world. Level II analysis moves beyond psychological frames to consider our social identities. In the academy, common social identity groups are racial, religious, ethnic, class, gender, and cultural, and the increasing heterogeneity of our faculty, student, and staff populations helps explain the increase of identity-based conflicts. Terms such as ethnocentrism, in- or out-groups, stereotypes, scapegoats, racism, and sexism all suggest aspects of social identity conflicts. These conflicts have common themes. Often there is evidence of personal accusations, threats, and retaliation. These conflicts escalate quickly. Parties seek allies with similar worldviews for support and, in doing so, may highlight the "evilness" of the other. When social identity-based conflicts occur, leaders need to move quickly. If it is possible to reframe the situation so that both parties can "save face," an intervention process is more likely to succeed.

Situation

When we consider situations, we are trying to understand factors of the parties' social contexts that may be influencing their behaviors. This includes the parties' *environment, time pressures, relationships with each other and with authority,* and *roles.* It also includes any perceived *opportunities for conversation* and *problem solving.* Do the parties believe there will be *repercussions?* Is there any negotiation flexibility? Does the behavior of the parties in the conflict remain fairly consistent in other contexts? Do the responses seem unusual? If there is little evidence that the parties involved engage in similar conflictual behavior most of the time or in other settings, it suggests that the situation needs greater exploration. Changing the situation may become the best intervention strategy.

The sociological and contextual issues of situations and identities (Level II) and social and psychological issues of types, sources, and dynamics (Level I) are usually nested in an even larger sociopolitical and structural context. This context is the third level of our conflict analysis.

LEVEL III ANALYSIS OF MACRO ISSUES: CULTURE, TRADITIONS, AND STRUCTURES

Macro issues influencing conflict are the social, organizational, political, and economic aspects of our environment. We consider such questions as:

- What is unique to our college or university?

- What are the *cultural aspects* of my college that help me understand this particular conflict? What are the *subcultures* (for example teaching versus research faculty, clinical versus regular faculty, administration versus staff) that exist?

- What traditions and structures are in place that support or enhance the conflict or that could be used to intervene?

- What are the *traditions, rules,* and *regulations* we want to consider that can and will escalate or deescalate the conflict?

Culture

The concept and study of culture in the social sciences is complex with many definitions. Unlike the popular concept of culture as the acquisition of artifacts, specialized knowledge, and other precious materials which say that people who accumulate these "have culture," social scientists define culture as the *laws, customs, belief systems,* and *language* people acquire. Our framework considers culture in the context of our colleges and universities and, specifically, the distinction between the *collegial* and the *managerial culture* about which Eugene Rice and Mary Deane Sorcinelli have written. Universities have a long history of collaboration based on peer accountability; merit, as the basis for promotion; and shared governance. But universities have shared two cultures, the collegial for the academics and the managerial for the nonacademics. Many colleges and universities are moving away from this dual approach to a managerial, hierarchical model. Does the conflict in the department reflect the folkways, mores, and belief systems of working collaboratively and co-operatively, respecting various voices? Or does it reflect a hierarchical culture where position power or status is the dominant factor in decision-making processes?

We know culture across groups within our colleges or across departments is not homogeneous, stable, or even. The collegial nature of the department can be more or less dominant in some areas and not in others, even within the nonacademic side of the institution. Conflict provides interesting insight and an opportunity to revisit departmental norms, especially if the conflict reflects norms and expectations deemed inappropriate behavior in the department (for example, use of contentious influence, creating hostile work environments, and unprofessional accusations).

Traditions

When we consider the larger context of traditions, we are talking about the *deeply rooted* and *persistent behaviors* in the university over a long period of time. Rice and Sorcinelli make an important distinction between the prestige economy, embedded in the collaborative culture, and the market economy, based on the managerial culture. In the prestige economy, status counts as currency. That includes credentials, ranking, and type of institution. It has a loose connection to the market economy in that an elite private liberal arts college (high status), for example, can get away with charging higher tuition than a college or university with less prestige. In the market economy, money counts as currency. That means programs need to be cost effective and staffing should be lean. For example, is it worth the money to upgrade software and the training to use it? The market drives decisions as to what programs are developed, rewarded, or eliminated. As institutional missions and visions change, traditions will follow, albeit much more slowly.

Structures

Organizations have characteristics that compel members to act in certain ways. We have discussed the impact of cultural norms and traditions on behavior. Structures of the academy are the *laws, policies, procedures,* and *rules* on campus and, specifically, the ways these encourage or impede conflict. For example, when our economy moves into a recession, university leaders may require departments to make across-the-board budget cuts. This is a structural intervention (rule) for solving budgetary problems, but one that will surely result in conflict. Another example is the institutionalization of assessment processes. Most campuses have relatively new offices of assessment responsible for assuring the public—legislators, trustees, accreditation agencies, parents, and current and prospective students—that the institution is doing what it says it is doing. These offices add to administrative costs and generate guidelines or rules as to what and how data will be collected and who should be responsible to do so. Conflicts result, varying from resentment because of added responsibilities or redirecting resources to outright hostility for imposed-upon requirements for change.

CONSIDERING INTERVENTIONS

The final section of this chapter anticipates Chapter Seven regarding possible interventions. A thorough diagnosis of the conflict—including an understanding of the types, sources, and dynamics of the conflict in the context of identity and situational issues, embedded in larger institutional traditions, culture, and structures—informs our thinking about what to do with the conflict. How can the academic administrator or manager resolve it?

The four most commonly used interventions are:

- *Negotiation:* At the heart of resolving all conflicts is some kind of negotiation process. Negotiation is a discussion between the two parties with a goal of settling their dispute.

- *Facilitation:* Usually called an *assisted negotiation,* facilitation is conducted by a third party, often the manager or leader. Facilitators create conditions to enhance discussion including opportunities to hear one another. The process addresses immediate concerns, hopes, and long-term goals.

- *Mediation:* An extension of the negotiation process, mediation involves a formal third party who has limited or no authority in making decisions and is neutral to the outcome of the conflict. Rather, the mediator helps disputants reach acceptable settlements by problem solving, transforming the relationship, or some combination of the two.

- *Arbitration:* Arbitration is the settlement of a dispute by a person who is selected to hear evidence and testimony from both sides, and then makes a binding or nonbinding decision or ruling, depending on the conditions of the arbitration.

Managers and leaders also have a variety of other third parties available at colleges to help with a conflict: personnel in human resources departments, counseling services, ombuds offices, diversity programs and services, disability resource centers, and university legal counsel are just a few. As you explore the various options, ask such questions as:

- How do I deal with this conflict?

- Is there room for negotiation?

- Do the parties need a better understanding of assumptions they are making about each other and the situation?

- Does this conflict warrant an outside third person such as a mediator, ombudsperson, or "behind-the-scenes" peacemaker?

- Is it time to seek legal counsel?

- Is an arbitrator the appropriate next step?

SUMMARY

We have presented a framework that involves three levels of analysis of any conflict: the micro, psychological components that include types, sources, and dynamics of the conflict; the influences and contexts of the meso-level social concerns that help us analyze ways in which the situation and the parties' identities impact the conflict; and the macro-level concerns that consider the influences of academic cultures and institutional traditions. A careful conflict analysis needs to precede any consideration of its resolution so as to make an informed match of an intervention strategy from an array of possibilities appropriate to the situation. Our hope is that as you progress through the book, the diagnostic process will get easier, understanding the complexities of conflict will seem less daunting, and a useful intervention strategy will seem obvious. We will provide you with opportunities to practice using the framework. Ultimately, we hope that when you encounter conflict that seems to take on "a life of its own" you will know how to unbundle it, sort out what is going on, and develop a plan to solve it.

3

Intrapersonal Conflict

The Impact of Stress and Negative Thinking

AT THIS POINT WE HAVE established the following: Conflict is a process in which one party perceives that its interests are being opposed by another party. Conflict is inevitable, but it need not be destructive. Creative conflict can improve problem solving, clarify decision making, and strengthen commitment. Preventing dysfunctional conflicts is the best way of handling dissension in a department. However, assessing when conflicts are headed in destructive directions requires leaders to be aware of pressures created by role conflicts; to be optimistic yet realistic in their thinking; to be self-confident; to have good communication and listening skills; and to be able to manage their own stress levels.

But what happens when conflict is occurring within ourselves? Internal conflict often disrupts our ability to correctly identify the real problem, contributes to misinterpretation of a situation, impedes our problem-solving ability, makes us indecisive, interferes with good communication, and impairs our listening skills. Internal conflict is more likely to occur when we are already feeling stressed. The three situations that can be frequent causes of stress in academic administrators are role conflict, role ambiguity, and role overload.

ROLE CONFLICT

Individuals who have family responsibilities are likely to experience conflict between the obligations that are required by their work and the problems that stem from their role as parents. Since both spouses in most of today's families with children are employed, both partners, as well as single parents, frequently have family commitments that conflict with their job responsibilities. How can supervisors juggle their own conflicting obligations? How much latitude should one of their employees be given when a child is ill and the regular sitter is unavailable? Or when an employee refuses to cover evening or weekend registration because she or he is needed at home? Or when faculty members refuse to teach at particular times because they need to be at home to take care of children or aging parents? How do other members of a department perceive any special allowances given to their colleagues because of family responsibilities?

Role conflict also occurs when a supervisor must serve as both evaluator and mentor to an employee who needs help in improving performance. While evaluation is often used in making judgments about performance as a basis for personnel decision making, mentoring is an ongoing, supportive process that focuses on an individual's personal and professional development. Evaluation and mentoring differ in terms of the relative weight they give to organizational and individual goals. When these goals conflict, what determines which side a supervisor should support?

ROLE AMBIGUITY

Role ambiguity occurs when an individual must represent the department to administration and must represent administration to department members or direct reports. For example, as universities cut staff to manage their budgets, or delay filling vacated employee slots to reduce expenditures, supervisors must often request that the remaining staff perform additional tasks that are not usually part of their job descriptions. One supervisor handled this by telling her department that "the department head made me do it." Another supervisor, however, told her department members, "Our university budget is really tight. We are not replacing employees who have left. All of the other departments in the university must do the same thing. This is a way to avoid cutting personnel. How would you suggest we handle the work formerly performed by the two people who have left?" While the first supervisor set up an adversarial relationship between her department head and the employees, the second supervisor turned the situation into a problem to be solved. Her employees would also be more likely to accept the final solution because they had made the decision.

ROLE OVERLOAD

Role overload and underload occur when employees are asked to do too much or too little. Role overload happens when an individual has too much work or when an individual doesn't have the skills or abilities to perform a given job. A new supervisor, who has been given too little training, can experience a high level of stress. Or in some jobs in which the quantity of work ebbs and flows, supervisors can experience stress in both the peak periods and in the times when work is slow. Routine work and too little work can result in stress that is triggered by boredom. In universities, which run on a semester or quarter basis, there are periods of high activity and times when things are slow. Being interrupted by students or faculty who have "an emergency that can only be handled by the administrator," or a call from the dean or director who wants to see you right away, can create role overload. When any of these stresses occurs in the roles we have, it sets up conflict. These are all conflicts that fragment an individual and must be handled if a leader is to survive. Employees and supervisors who believe they have the understanding and help from the person to whom they report handle high levels of stress more effectively than those who do not have such support. Supervisors need to be aware of the effect such stressful periods have on employees and provide the help and support they need before their morale is affected.

NEGATIVE THINKING

Role conflict, ambiguity, and overload certainly create stress and internal conflicts. In addition, psychological research and comparative outcome studies on therapeutic interventions demonstrate that individuals' tendency to think positively or negatively impacts their perceptions of themselves and others. Negative and positive thoughts are called cognitions and include self-talk, the labels we put on people and events, and the myths and assumptions under which we operate. In 1976 Aaron Beck wrote the first book for psychotherapists on the effect of negative thinking, an approach that made a monumental impact on psychology and psychotherapy. In the 1990s Martin E. P. Seligman wrote three popular books on the impact of optimism and positive psychology, demonstrating for the reader how to replace pessimistic thinking with optimistic thought. These are helpful for academic administrators as they deal with negative people and indeed with their own negative thinking.

When we present an idea to negative thinkers, they will tell us what's wrong with the concept, why it will never work, and particularly why it can't be implemented in this institution. However, if we are willing to listen to them and get past their negativity, perhaps even ask them if there is anything good about the idea, or how they would prefer to solve the problem, they may realize that what is being suggested has some merit and agree that what we are offering is a viable option, or at least that they can't come up with a better solution. They may accept what we have told them or make some adjustments that we can live with while still implementing the basic idea with which we began. Listening and demonstrating that we value their thinking and their right to have a different point of view are effective ways to handle negative thinkers. Chapter Five on intragroup conflict includes more information on how to handle faculty members or employees who are negative thinkers, particularly those who are often labeled "difficult."

How Our Negative Thoughts Affect Us

It is important for academic administrators to be aware of the characteristics and effects of negative thinking.

- Negative thoughts trigger anxiety, helplessness, and depression.

- Negative thoughts are automatic.

- We are not usually aware that we are thinking negatively.

- Negative thoughts usually begin with a fact, but move on to inferences that are not necessarily true. Once we draw the conclusion, we respond to it as if it were engraved in stone.

- There may be a dozen different conclusions we can draw from a fact, but negative thinkers tend to make a deduction that puts themselves in a negative light, or is downright catastrophic.

- Negative thinking is learned and, therefore, can be unlearned.

Dealing with Negative Thinking in Ourselves

We can counteract the effects of negative thinking by turning negative irrational thoughts into positive realistic thinking. This can be done by using a process called cognitive restructuring. Think of the last time that you found yourself procrastinating. The following example shows how negative thinking can lead to procrastination and how positive realistic thinking can unblock the paralysis.

Your self-talk may sound like this: "An important project which will determine whether we get what we need for the department has been assigned to me. It will take a long stretch of time to complete it. If I rush, I won't do it right. I will tackle it next week when I have finished some of these other things on my desk." But next week comes and goes and you have not yet started the project.

How do you handle this so you don't procrastinate? First, understand the dynamics of procrastination. Your self-message is, "Working on the project in question makes me feel anxious. I'm not sure I can write the report so that it will have the effect I am hoping for. If this happens, I will let down my department and the person to whom I report will be disappointed in me." You need to change the message so that it is more realistic. Constructive self-talk, combined with a problem-solving approach, might sound like this: "This is an important project and I want to do it well. I will divide the project into its logical parts. Then I will know which areas require additional information. I can ask my secretary or assistant to gather that information so that I will have it ready when I need it. I will set time lines that allow a sufficient period for the information to be entered in the computer and for me to review it. I will allocate an hour a day to work on small portions of the report and not let anything keep me from doing it. I will feel really satisfied when I can give this report to the person to whom I report because it will provide the basis for her approving what I need for the department for the next year."

Notice the steps involved:

1. Break the large (overwhelming) project into small manageable parts.

2. Plan and schedule how and when each part will be completed. Don't let yourself be interrupted during the time you have set aside to work on the project. Discontinuing work on what is uncomfortable or anxiety-provoking is a reward. Recognize the tendency to redirect your efforts to more enjoyable activities. Anxiety goes down when you stop to talk on the telephone, or have a cup of coffee with a colleague. This is equivalent to rewarding yourself for avoidance. The psychological term for this activity is *negative reinforcement* (the reward that occurs when something painful stops, or the termination of an aversive stimulus, namely, anxiety).

3. Delegate those parts that you don't have to do yourself. Celebrate the completion of each part, even if this simply means mentally patting yourself on the back. What will doom completion of the project is to punish yourself for what you accomplish. For example, "Yes, I have finished that part, but I have so much more to do. I'll never get it completed by the deadline." Success and a feeling of accomplishment increase the probability that you will return to this work as soon as the next scheduled time approaches: "That's great. I've done exactly what I planned to do, that is, spend an hour on this project today." When what you have to do is unpleasant or difficult, reward yourself for time spent, not for what you have accomplished.

If you begin to recognize a tendency to think negatively, try this approach, which is another method of cognitive restructuring, or changing those negative thoughts to positive ones. As soon as you start to feel uncomfortable (your early warning signal), try to identify your negative thoughts. Then ask yourself, "What evidence is there for this statement? What evidence is there against it?" Or, relive a recent experience in which you were successful and savor it. The use of such an approach helps restore self-confidence. An example: Carol is an adviser, though not a faculty member, to the Executive MBA students who meet for their classes on Saturdays from 8:30 A.M. to 4:30 P.M. She has a positive, upbeat attitude toward her work, which comes from a recognition that she sometimes says to herself, "I'm in a bind. There is nothing that can be done about this situation." She then substitutes the message, "I have a problem, but I'm a good problem solver, so let me see what I can do about this." By now, she has become quite adept at using this approach. She has made a sign, which she has placed on her office door that says, "The good things that happen in this program are planned. The bad things are accidental."

This is how she has handled a recent problem. The Student Health Service Center is trying to satisfy a State Health Department requirement that health forms and immunization records for all students be filed in its office. If some of these forms are missing, the department places a "medical hold" on student records. This means that Carol cannot register them. If there is a "medical hold," students may miss out on registering in time to begin a semester, which in turn means that the university will collect no tuition. The students are angry because the Student Health Center will not tell them what is missing. Because they are all adults, they feel that these immunization requirements do not apply to them. When Carol contacts the Student Health Services Center, they will not tell her what records are missing because, they say, it is a matter of students' privacy. The Health Center supervisor says that students were told in a letter when they first were accepted what documents were needed, and the employees don't have time to look up individual student records.

Being both knowledgeable about the structure of the university and also an effective problem solver, Carol knew that courses offered in the conference center on campus, which had originally been built for use in holding conferences and continuing education courses for businesses and other organizations in the community, was considered to be an off-campus center. People who took classes there were not required to provide health and immunization records. So, with permission of the provost, Carol simply switched all classes for the Executive MBA students to the conference center. Students were thus able to register for and take classes on time.

The students were happy that an annoying barrier had been removed, the university received its tuition, and the program was able to continue without this kind of problem.

Another example of Carol's problem-solving ability occurred on a freezing Saturday morning when individuals from the Food Services Department did not appear on campus. The MBA students were always provided with breakfast free-of-charge, the thinking being that if students got up early on Saturday to make an 8:30 A.M. class, they might not have time for breakfast. However, on this particular cold morning, when students were looking forward to a hot cup of coffee, no food was being served. Carol felt this was unacceptable. She called the home of the Food Services supervisor who told her that the person in charge was ill and not able to be on campus. Carol then telephoned the dean and asked his permission to buy breakfast herself. When he agreed, she asked a local Dunkin' Donuts to immediately deliver dozens of donuts and hot beverages. She put this purchase on her own credit card, knowing that she would be reimbursed. A negative thinker might simply have explained what had happened to the students and bad-mouthed the supervisor of Food Services.

Dealing with Negative Thinking in Others

Sometimes negative thinkers can become a toxic influence in an entire department. For example, in one department in which there are four employees in Accounts Payable (student refunds) and four in Student Loans (student refunds, student repayment, and collection), the unit has been structured and operations have been set up to help minimize destructive conflict. All government updates are discussed at meetings that are held regularly. Also, this is an informal organization, so people feel free to go to another individual to ask questions. The department meets for educational seminars. Procedures are all written down to prevent conflicts. The frequent meetings and written procedures update everyone on government regulations. People in the department get along well together because there is no need to argue about different interpretations of regulations.

Within the past month, a new person has joined the department. The new member is difficult. She makes personal attacks at meetings and frequently gives two or three reasons why any new idea won't work. With their past experience of getting along well together, the members of the department seem reluctant to confront her and don't have the skills or experience to challenge her directly.

There are a number of ways that the department head can handle this situation. The department head can

- Set a rule with the group that they must discuss the positive aspects of all new ideas before discussing any negatives.

- Capture all negative ideas on a separate flip chart so that the new employee will feel that her ideas have registered with the group. (People often become louder or more negative when they feel their ideas have not been listened to.)

- Reinforce the rules of brainstorming, that is, no positive or negative judgments may be made until many ideas are on the table.

- Use a meetings audit, which is a two-minute appraisal of the things participants liked or disliked about the meeting.

- Try a stop action, which says, "Stop action. This is what I observe we are doing. Is this what we want to be doing?"

- Paraphrase what the negative employee says in more positive terms, make eye contact, and smile at her when speaking. Don't let her alienate herself from the group.

Errors in Negative Thinking

Finally, there are two major assumptions that can paralyze us: the *fundamental attribution error* and the *self-serving bias*. The fundamental attribution error is the tendency to underestimate the significance of external causes of behavior and to overestimate internal causes of behavior in order to understand when individuals fail in what they do. For example, a supervisor, who had just been promoted to the position, blamed his group's low productivity on their laziness (internal causes) and did not recognize that there was no accountability built into the system (external causes). By placing the emphasis on internal factors in others, the new supervisor felt helpless to do anything about the situation because he felt stymied by the union contract, which set minimal standards of work to be accomplished. He felt conflicted because he wanted to accomplish what he had been hired to do, but didn't see any way of achieving his goals. The solution would have been to look at, and change, some of the external factors in the department that perpetuated employee behavior, such as the lack of accountability.

Another example is of a faculty member who recognized external factors in her department instead of simply blaming others. This woman worked in a department where there was little collegiality or support for one another and in which the department chair felt no responsibility for creating a sense of community. She had just had a book published, and although her picture appeared on the cover of the alumni magazine, not a single person in the department congratulated her on her accomplishment. Although she valued the recognition she was getting from others outside the university, she was unhappy that none of her colleagues had acknowledged her work. She decided to do something about it. She brought a few bottles of wine to the department meeting and said to her colleagues, "My book was just published last week. I knew you would want to celebrate with me, so I brought some wine." Obviously, everyone had to congratulate her, and she could feel satisfied that her work had been recognized by members of her department, even though she made it happen herself. And hopefully, she drew from her colleagues some supportive behavior that the department chair could see was desirable.

The other frequent assumption is the *self-serving bias,* which is a tendency for individuals to credit their own success to internal factors, such as their ability or effort, and to attribute their failures to external factors, such as task difficulty or luck. While accepting responsibility for one's own good performance can lead to further success, the tendency to deny any responsibility for one's own poor performance often contributes to a feeling of helplessness in changing others' behavior.

An example of using the self-serving bias to explain one's personal failure occurred when a supervisor decided that he should sponsor ongoing training sessions for people in his department to increase their knowledge and skills. At a workshop for the employees, he asked them what topics they would like covered at a series of meetings he would sponsor. "Raising salaries" was the first response given. Two or three other individuals agreed. A second person offered the topic of "filling the vacancies in the department so we won't be so overworked." Instead of agreeing that these were real problems over which he had little control, and then trying to elicit other topics that interested them, he ended the meeting and left.

When he returned to his office, the manager decided that meetings with employees in that department would be unproductive and dropped the entire plan. This was destructive because (1) he had raised their expectations when he told them he planned to have meetings to discuss problems they were encountering, (2) he blamed them for coming up with topics he felt he could do nothing about, although he did not give them any feedback about his reaction to the suggestions, and (3) just dropping the project would create an adversarial relationship with them. If instead, he had interviewed several informal leaders in the group for the purpose of determining their needs, and then written a letter to all of the department members listing an array of topics and indicating where the list had come from, this episode could have had an entirely different outcome. However, the manager accepted no responsibility for what had happened and externalized the blame by telling himself that the employees were being unrealistic and manipulative. This is the self-serving bias at its worst.

SUMMARY

When conflict occurs within academic administrators, it can immobilize them. The first step in preventing intra-individual conflict is to recognize that particular kinds of stress (role conflict, role ambiguity, and role overload) can exacerbate internal conflict. Second, become aware that negative thinking often results in feelings of helplessness, anxiety, depression, and sometimes hostile behavior. Self-confidence is diminished, and the incentive to carry out implementation steps in the achievement of goals disappears. Keep in mind our tendency to take credit for accomplishments and to externalize the blame for failures. Develop a good supportive relationship, perhaps with a colleague or director from another department with whom you can celebrate accomplishments, talk freely, and not be concerned that he or she will break confidence. Finally, using some of the strategies suggested in this chapter, such as substituting positive rational thinking for negative self-talk, and then evaluating the outcomes when this different approach is used, will counteract the barriers that stand in the way of successful leadership and management of conflict.

4

Interpersonal Conflict

Helping People Who Don't Get Along

ALTHOUGH ACADEME AS an ivory tower is a common stereotype, there are many chinks in the structure and many dysfunctional behaviors among its inhabitants. In some departments, conflict creates so much tension that people hate to come to work. In others, individuals, when interviewed, will say that everybody gets along very well and that they never even have a disagreement. Although the latter sounds idyllic, there may well be a number of unresolved issues that have simply gone underground because conflict can be so unpleasant. Some individuals have fragile egos, and when others in a department seem to ignore a recommendation they have made, they isolate themselves and pull out of all departmental activities. Others don't ask them what the problem is, and they don't volunteer that information, and soon it is taken for granted that they simply do not participate. So the task of the supervisor or director is to prevent destructive conflict or to turn dysfunctional conflict into conflict that is constructive. Although task-oriented people often focus primarily on getting the problem solved, an effective outcome can't be claimed unless a good relationship between the parties has been preserved.

FOUR BASIC OUTCOMES OF INTERPERSONAL CONFLICT

Any conflicts between two or more people can have four possible outcomes. Keeping in mind the importance of resolving the problem while maintaining a good relationship will help avoid creating a win-lose approach.

- *The problem is resolved, and the relationship is maintained or even improved.* This results when each individual is treated with respect and each feels the other understands her or his point of view. The problem is resolved because each of the two people has expressed her or his perspective, needs, and goals in a manner that is not judgmental or accusatory. The other party simply uses active listening or paraphrasing without being defensive.

- *The problem is not resolved, and the relationship deteriorates because of personal attacks.* This happens when one of the parties disrespects the other by minimizing the importance of the problem, or denigrates the other individual as not being entitled to any special treatment.

- *The problem is solved, but the relationship is eroded.* This results when one individual insists that his or her solution must be the one chosen and has enough power to enforce this viewpoint.

- *The problem is not solved, but the relationship is maintained or gets even better.* This happens when both parties recognize that the problem cannot be solved with the resources or time available. However, because of the way each has behaved, and what they have learned about problem solving, both parties feel that their perspective is valued and they feel affirmed.

Recognizing that it is critical to maintain a good relationship between two individuals—and not just solve the problem—often keeps people from developing grudges that occur when people not only don't get what they wanted but feel the process used to deal with the issue was unfair.

WHEN DOES INTERPERSONAL CONFLICT OCCUR?

As Clyde H. Coombs wrote in the mid-1980s, there are two sets of circumstances in which conflict is likely to occur. *Conflict can happen when two people want the same thing but must settle for different things.* For example, what happens when two people in the same department want to take their vacations during the same two weeks? The department is already short-staffed because one person is out on disability and another is on a three-month maternity leave. A supervisor can meet with each individual separately to find out why he or she cannot take a different vacation period, then conduct a three-way meeting to enable each person to appreciate the other's perspective. Sometimes one of the two people will be able to suggest a way of resolving the conflict, some sort of trade-off or other benefit offered to the individual who accommodates the other. Only when the two people cannot come to an agreement does the supervisor step in and make a decision, offering something to sweeten the agreement, or using some criterion such as seniority.

Conflict can also occur when people want different things but must settle for the same thing. What happens when a technology department wants to subsume a center for teaching and learning under its jurisdiction, and the center wants to remain as an independent unit? If a new structure is imposed, neither department will be completely satisfied unless its goal is achieved. Yet, people in both departments have complementary skills. The use of technology in education needs to be informed by individuals who are sophisticated about course design, teaching, and assessment methodology. Moreover, teaching and learning centers profit from sophisticated knowledge about the use of technology in the classroom. The individuals who lead each department may become codirectors of the new unit, or be able to agree on the best way to merge their combination of knowledge and skills. The people involved can revisit the decision in six months, or sooner, to tackle any problems that emerge.

In either type of conflict, if self-interests overshadow mutual interests, the likelihood is that each individual will attempt to use power instead of collaboration or compromise to resolve the issue. And in either circumstance, if the bond between the people in conflict is not strong, the relationship will significantly deteriorate. For a director or supervisor, the task is to preserve departmental stability, which cannot exist when individuals are alienated from one another, which can then become clique against clique. In addition to being aware that they must pay attention to the final outcome, department heads must be aware that under usual circumstances conflict does not suddenly erupt. There are warning signs. When academic leaders are aware of such indicators, they can intervene more quickly and effectively to head off serious problems.

STAGES OF CONFLICT

There is sometimes a long history of conflict between two members of the same department. Knowing that conflict often occurs in stages helps the director recognize the importance of intervention in the early phases where conflict is more manageable and before it escalates and fragments a department. In the late 1960s L. R. Pondy described five stages of conflict: (1) latent conflict, (2) perceived conflict, (3) felt conflict, (4) manifest conflict, and (5) conflict aftermath. The following example not only illustrates how conflict can increase over time but also shows how the problem and the relationship become so intertwined that effective resolution is almost impossible.

The position of dean of students was open. Peter and Dan, both internal candidates, applied for the job. Peter believed that as associate dean of students, he had more relevant experience than either Dan or the external candidates on the list. Dan felt that he had better academic credentials than Peter, that past evaluations of his performance were above average, and that, unlike the external candidates, he knew the university culture. It seemed apparent that the greatest competition would be between the two internal candidates. A *latent* stage of conflict, the phase in which conditions for conflict exist, had now been created.

A search and screen committee recommended Peter, the associate dean, as their first choice, and the provost appointed him to the position of dean of students. Now the position of associate dean of students was open, and Dan applied for it. Peter, the new dean, did not want to hire Dan, the only internal candidate and the one who had been placed on the short list by the search and screen committee. Peter believed that since Dan had not been chosen as dean of students, if Dan were made associate dean of students, this would create animosity between them. He also felt that Dan was sloppy in his work habits and not detail oriented, which the job required. When Peter interviewed Dan, and made some of his observations clear, conflict between the two arose to the *perceived* level.

Since Dan was a strong internal candidate, and despite the new dean's strong objections, the provost appointed him associate dean of students. Rather quickly, as Dan and Peter worked on projects together, it became apparent that the arrangement was not working. When, for example, Dan handled Freshman Orientation badly, he said he had received no guidance from Peter, who had performed this function several times. Instead, after the fact, Peter told him, "I wouldn't have done it that way." The conflict had now risen to the *felt* level.

Both men told the provost that they hated to come to work. Peter, who was now bothered by insomnia, headaches, difficulty concentrating, heart pounding, diarrhea, and mild depression, showed all of the symptoms of *manifest* conflict. He then took a medical leave of absence, and Dan became the interim dean. The people in his unit began to report that his work "was a disaster." He was asked by the provost to submit a monthly report, but Dan did not turn one in. When reminded, he turned in two reports at the end of two months. The provost told Dan the reports were not very strong and did not include many of the activities he was supposed to accomplish. All of Peter's misgivings turned out to be true.

Peter, now returned from his medical leave, was asked to submit monthly reports, which he did faithfully. Although the provost believed that Peter lacked vision, nevertheless, at a final meeting the provost terminated Dan because he felt Dan's performance was incompetent. Dan was very angry and said that his job performance had been excellent, and indeed his evaluations showed above average performance. The situation had now reached the stage of conflict *aftermath*. Since Dan's performance evaluations were above average, the provost was concerned that Dan might sue the university, which did not happen but could have.

One of the questions the provost now asks is, "What could have prevented this situation from occurring?" Clearly, several interventions could have been considered. Since Peter objected so strongly to Dan's appointment as associate dean, based on the gap between what the job required (willingness to seek and accept direction, good work habits, and being detail oriented) and fairly objective observations of Dan's performance, which did not include these characteristics, Dan should not have been placed in this position.

However, once Dan had been hired, a few constructive things could have been done. Dan had excellent people skills, an ability that Peter lacked. If they had been able to work together, their skills could have supplemented each other's to create strengths in the dean of students office. This would require that the provost meet with them, indicate that the new team required training, and appoint someone to help them collaborate from the beginning. The provost asked the question, "Does the university assume responsibility for training senior managers?" The answer is yes, particularly when conflict can be anticipated. It is not realistic to simply throw two people together and hope that they will learn to cooperate. Much grief could have been avoided if this step had been taken. Vision and mission statements, goals, implementation steps, and time lines needed to be set up and cleared with the provost. Accountability could have been built in by Peter and Dan giving monthly reports of goal accomplishments (which the provost did implement, though not from the beginning), and if they had not been reached, to use a form of mid-stream correction, that is, adjusting the implementation steps by changing what was necessary so that the goals could be reached. Weekly meetings could have been set up, the dean could have been taught how to give the associate dean more direction, and their job descriptions could have been rewritten to capitalize on the strengths of each person. This situation was also ripe for an intervention from an ombudsperson or other third party intervention strategies, which are discussed in Chapter Seven.

SKILLS NEEDED FOR CONFLICT RESOLUTION

There are several important elements in managing conflict successfully. These factors are essential whether you are dealing with interpersonal conflict between two people or disagreement within a department.

1. *Manage your anger.* Recognize that when you feel your competence or judgment is being questioned, or that someone is deliberately trying to block the achievement of your goals, you feel denigrated. If you feel helpless because you don't know how to right the wrongs, you feel like a child and must do something to regain your equilibrium. That may mean demonstrating your power through criticism or threat, raising your voice, or using sarcasm. But any of these approaches escalates the conflict and rarely leads to resolution of a problem.

2. *Use active listening.* Paraphrase what you hear the other person saying, in terms of both the words used and the emotions being expressed: "I understand you are really angry about this" or "I can see that this is very important to you." Your purpose is to show the other individual that you are willing to try to comprehend her point of view, help both of you understand what goals you have in common, and what just ways there are of helping both of you achieve your goals. If the achievement of one set of goals negates the possibility of accomplishing the other, at least try to find a way to resolve the issue that both of you agree is fair. For example, take turns, or give the other something he or she wants instead.

3. *Avoid making assumptions.* Because we cannot read minds, we can never really know why someone did something. Some of us tend to be negative thinkers who automatically assume the worst in an ambiguous situation. Instead of giving the other person the benefit of the doubt, we conclude that if the other person really valued us, she or he would meet our expectations. This can occur even when we haven't verbalized what these expectations are. Assumptions can be checked by paraphrasing what we hear and by asking questions to clarify the meaning of what someone else has said.

4. *Discover the nugget of gold in what the other individual is saying.* What can you find that you can honestly agree with? Affirm it and show the other person that you value her or his right to have a different perspective from your own.

5. *Remember that criticism is explosive and must always be handled sensitively.* You need to ask yourself: When was the last time that criticism changed someone else's behavior? What is the probable effect that criticism will have on another's behavior? Using criticism effectively is a

special skill. If it is done poorly, it can hurt a relationship more than it can help. This is not to say that criticism should never be used, only that it needs to focus on the behavior to be changed rather than blaming or accusing.

6. *Learn the skills of negotiation and problem solving.* Chapter Seven discusses further when and how these skills and other third party intervention approaches can be used effectively.

7. *Develop a good support network.* Supervisors and directors often feel "alone in the trenches." If promoted from within a department, they can no longer confide in individuals who are former coworkers. Reluctant to "wash dirty linen in public," they do not want to discuss department problems with people outside the department. So the task is to find someone else in the university to talk to, someone whom they can trust to keep a confidence and to give them good advice.

Most individuals have not been trained to be successful in conflict resolution, either as part of their academic preparation or in their personal development. People have been trained to be critical of other perspectives, to be skillful in defending their own professional and personal points of view, and to function most effectively in isolation. Many people have not learned how to make interpersonal conflict productive. A supervisor of a department, therefore, often finds that two department members who are competing for the same—often limited—resources will indicate what they want, and if they don't get it, will try to enlist other people in their cause. They may offer arguments of seniority, educational background, political correctness, or simply moral rectitude to bolster their positions. Sometimes they will go to a dean or provost to complain. Occasionally, they will write memos to the president with copies to everyone else in the administrative hierarchy.

Because conflict can be so unpleasant, it is frequently avoided. However, if its cause has not been resolved it occasionally erupts at a department meeting in an abrasive fashion, in sarcastic remarks, or in a particularly venomous statement to or about a colleague. Often, those who witness such behavior become uncomfortable and resolve privately to find ways of preventing similar outbursts from occurring again. From all of this, it is clear that a supervisor or director cannot allow conflict to escalate to the point where it erodes and fragments relationships in a department. Conflict must be managed, although it cannot always be resolved.

Dealing with conflict constructively also includes the ability and willingness to speak directly to the person with whom you are having a problem. When we have conducted team-building projects for departments and ask people to make a list of problems they might encounter in the department and how they can resolve them, they typically include the solution of "no backstabbing," which they explain is a frequent cause of conflict in their departments. They usually go on to suggest: "If you are angry with someone, don't complain to someone else." Examples are when someone is not cleaning up after herself after using a piece of equipment, or not doing her share when working on a project or committee, or denigrating someone to a department head, or withholding information that someone needs to do a job. "Go directly to the person with whom you are upset and problem-solve" is their solution.

Once an interpersonal conflict becomes personalized, individuals may experience gastrointestinal problems, insomnia, or tension headaches. They begin to make assumptions about the "enemy," believing the other is mean-spirited, vindictive, deliberately hurtful, or arrogant. However, if the person engages in the defensive or malicious behavior assumed to be true of the other party, she may justify it by saying "I was pushed into it" and "I had to protect my interests." In the process, many erroneous assumptions develop that need to be clarified before the conflict can be resolved.

TURNING A CONFLICT INTO A PROBLEM TO BE RESOLVED

The first step in resolving a problem is to identify the symptoms. In the example given earlier in this chapter about the dean of students office, the symptoms of the problem were physiological signs of stress in Peter and his need to request a medical leave. In addition, Dan's poor handling of

Freshman Orientation and his not satisfying the provost's request to submit a monthly progress report were symptoms that a problem existed.

The second step for parties in a conflict is to define and reframe the problem. In this case, the problem might be how to make Student Services a more productive department. Although these steps may be handled by the two people involved in the conflict, making use of a facilitator (a third party) can make a significant difference. Once people learn what is involved in facilitation, that is, helping each other to appreciate the perspective of the other person, they can appoint a facilitator in their own department. The process is for parties to state their perspective, one at a time, including their goals. After the first party verbalizes his or her point of view, the second party simply uses nondefensive active listening or paraphrasing until the speaker agrees that the points are understood. If not accurately heard, the speaker repeats what she has said until the listener paraphrases it to the satisfaction of the speaker. As the two individuals take turns doing this, each one understands better the viewpoint of the other. Misperceptions are clarified, and the problem is identified more objectively.

When people have the skills for constructive problem solving, they can more easily turn conflicts into problems to be resolved. Part of the responsibility of each individual in the chain of command is to develop the people who report to him or her. Providing opportunities for people to learn to solve conflicts effectively can be an important personal and professional development experience. If individuals feel incapable of resolving conflicts on their own, or if the conflict will consume more time than an individual wants to invest, an ombudsperson can be appointed from within the department. In one situation, an individual felt strongly that women should not hold any key leadership positions at the college and refused to take women seriously. Conflicts between this person and others were ongoing, and students often lined up outside the director's office to complain about being treated unjustly. Since the person refused to speak with the department head about the problem, a highly regarded ex-administrator in the department was appointed by the head as an ombudsman to help resolve the conflicts. In other instances, a facilitator can be invited to the department from some other part of the university to serve that function on a temporary basis. Some universities have people in the Human Resource Management Department who have skills in this area.

Once the symptoms of the problem have been identified and the problem has been defined through reframing, the remaining steps in problem solving are fairly straightforward:

1. Generate many alternative solutions.

2. List and weigh the pros and cons of all viable options.

3. Select an alternative both parties can live with.

4. Experiment by trying the solution for a designated period of time.

5. Define the criteria to be used in evaluating the effectiveness of the alternative.

6. If the solution works or can be tinkered with to make it work, agree to continue it for an indefinite period of time.

As possible conflict prevention, it generally helps for members of a department to make a list of anticipated conflicts and how they should be resolved. Such a statement can be included as a policy statement for the departmental handbook. Then, when that particular problem surfaces, there is an objective document that everyone has developed, and to which all have agreed, that can be used to solve the problem. In a student loans department, the entire group meets regularly to discuss changes in federal regulations. These changes are included in the procedures manual. This provides consistent ways to handle problems as they arise, thus minimizing conflicts. Also, a library services office identified university-wide and departmental events requiring senior staff to be present. They created a year-long calendar with dates, responsibilities, and a list of who would represent the office. When a complication arises so that someone is unable to take his or her turn, it is easy to "trade" and all members know what is required of them.

In any interpersonal conflict, both individuals need to save face, which happens when people feel that their opinions are listened to and when both the content and emotions of their message are understood, usually through paraphrasing. Feeling that others are taking them seriously affirms their right to have an opinion, to be listened to, and to be taken seriously. Paraphrasing does not mean agreement. It means only that the listener is trying to fully understand the speaker's position. Nonjudgmental listening, or active listening as it is often called, is the single most important tool in handling conflict effectively. It also refers to understanding each part of another's perspective without being defensive, knowing that you will have an opportunity to fully express your own point of view.

SUMMARY

This chapter discussed the four basic outcomes of conflict, the circumstances that provoke conflict, the five stages of conflict, when interventions are most likely to be helpful, and the skills needed for conflict resolution. The steps involved in identifying a problem and reframing it so that it becomes a problem to be solved, instead of a cause of dysfunctional conflict, are important skills for an academic administrator to cultivate. When the skills needed for conflict resolution are practiced, the leader will find that competence in handling conflict well can also be an important professional development experience.

5

Intragroup Conflict

The Academic Administrator as Team Leader

WE NOW TURN TO INTRAGROUP conflict that occurs among members of a department or a unit. While it is true that many of the quarrels in a department may be interpersonal, or between two people, this chapter deals with some of the specific intragroup conflicts that surface within a department. The very thought of conflict triggers anxiety, and indeed individuals in departments in which conflict is rampant have said that they can't sleep the night before a meeting. When conflict deteriorates into shouting matches and personal accusations, it can fragment a department. Department members can usually identify in advance who will cause the conflict. Departmental culture can also push conflict underground so that it is never dealt with. When this happens, tension is palpable, and although the relations between colleagues can appear congenial, the issues that divide them are never allowed to surface and be treated as problems to be resolved or as an opportunity to stimulate the generation of new ideas and energize behavior. When the leader of the group does not handle conflict well, it drains the energy of department members and can become so destructive it interferes with accomplishing any of the department's goals. When we look at intragroup conflict, we must look first at the norms that have evolved within a department to deal—or not to deal—with conflict.

DEPARTMENTAL NORMS

There is an old maxim in organizations that says, "If it ain't broke, don't fix it." But an effective leader engages in an ongoing quest for quality, looking for opportunities to make things better, whether or not they are obviously broken. In higher education, as in most organizations, the way people function is a result of both formal and informal rules and procedures that their group follows. These rules and procedures are the norms that guide individual behavior and have evolved over time from the departmental culture. The norms that evolve from the culture are typically not written down but are evident in such statements as, "In this department, it is all right to . . . ," or "Something like that would never work in a place like this": statements that indicate a strong norm that would be hard to change. Norms also guide how individuals handle conflict and whether a leader can effectively confront a department member who is causing conflict by demanding special privileges because of seniority or not sharing information with others who may need it.

Department members may be only dimly aware of the existence of some norms, so the department head must bring these norms to the individuals' attention. For example, once the department has confronted the norm of keeping conflict suppressed, disagreement can be used to make more effective decisions and reduce departmental tensions. Particularly when norms, or ground rules, have not been talked about in some time, or when a new individual becomes director, a department needs to discuss these issues:

- What is our main purpose?

- How can we best accomplish our mission and what ground rules will help us achieve our goals?

- How can we make our performance even better?

- How do we communicate with each other, both individually and in a group?

- Should we invite someone to attend one of our meetings as a process observer?

- How will we make decisions?

- How will we resolve problems?

- What kind of climate do we want in our group and how can we build that kind of climate?

Taking time to discuss these issues is part of the leader's responsibility, since these questions are basic to a group's effective functioning. Yet because some of the answers may appear obvious, people may resist even discussing these questions. However, once discussion begins, department members discover that the answers are far from obvious and that a team that sets clear ground rules can prevent many problems from occurring. Discussions can also ferret out the existence of negative norms, which can then be confronted and changed. Moreover, exploration of ways the department members want to function can result in commitment to a method of proceeding when dysfunctional conflict erupts.

STRATEGIES FOR MANAGING INTRAGROUP CONFLICT

More than three decades ago Kenneth W. Thomas identified five strategies for handling conflict. These concepts, which have been used by others with variations in language, are avoidance, accommodation, power, compromise or negotiation, and collaboration. The following examples illustrate events and interventions that can be generalized to any department or unit within the college or university.

Avoidance

In *avoidance,* which is characterized by physical or emotional withdrawal, the existence of a conflict is recognized, but the issues are not confronted. In one case, in meetings conducted by the director, participants avoided confronting two members of the group who seemed to enjoy treating serious topics on the agenda humorously. Each one played off the comments of the other and continued the humor for two or three minutes. Although their behavior was quite disruptive, neither the new director, who ran the meetings, nor the other supervisors ever confronted the two culprits. The director, who wanted to be viewed as flexible and empathic—unlike the previous administrator, who was thought to be fairly rigid—allowed this behavior to continue. The other department members simply waited until the two stopped engaging in this behavior and then went on with their meeting. Only when an outside consultant was brought in and said, "This group has an agenda, but I find that your jokes are getting us off track. Does anyone else feel this way?" every hand in the room shot up. The two individuals now realized that their colleagues were not amused, apologized, and stopped their disruptive behavior. However, unless the behavior had been confronted and peer pressure used, the problem would not have been solved and would have continued to occur. An outside consultant is not necessarily needed. Any member of the group can use the same intervention, although it is useful to ask one other influential person in the group for support before the meeting.

Accommodation

In *accommodation,* an individual tries to preserve harmony at all costs. Usually, this involves sacrificing an individual's own interests and needs in order to satisfy others. Sometimes department heads will emphasize their "serving" the department to the extent that they spend a disproportionate amount of time trying to please all of its members. Although in the short term things may run smoothly, in the long term the director may feel disappointed when department members do not accept their share of responsibility. Accommodation is a useful strategy when an individual doesn't have a heavy investment in the issue or feels that "I will have money in his bank so that he is more likely to let me have what I want the next time." However, this may not happen, and the person who has been so obliging gets tired of constantly giving in and may behave aggressively during the next encounter.

Power

A third strategy for managing conflict is *power.* The individual sets up a win-lose situation, and formal rules are often used to accomplish what that person wants. In one unit, which was made up of five separate departments, the director always introduced change and overcame objections by stating, "This is the way the vice president wants it to be handled." In this way, he never had to accept responsibility for the change and still got what he wanted. The department heads couldn't resent the director because they thought he had no input into the new policy or procedures. This arrangement lasted for about two years until others in the departments realized what he was doing. When they went to the vice president to complain that some of the new policies created some serious problems and documented what they were saying, he told them that he would inform all of the directors that any policy changes would now be issued in writing and distributed to all department heads and employees. Nevertheless, power is a legitimate strategy in an emergency, when a deadline must be met, when a rationale is provided for the change, or when members of the department have no investment in the issue.

Negotiation or Compromise

Negotiation, or *compromise,* is the first of the five strategies that considers the needs of both parties. In negotiation, each person is willing to give up some of what he or she wants in order to gain something else. Negotiation is the most frequently used approach when staff contracts are being settled and works when both parties are willing to give up something that has a lower priority for them. The disadvantage of this approach is that people often remember what it was they had to give up to get what they wanted and feel resentful. This may trigger other conflicts. When staff in an Enrollment Management unit agreed to work two extra hours at night and one day on the weekend during peak periods in exchange for equivalent time off, staff members felt taken advantage of and became resentful.

Collaboration

In *collaboration,* the last conflict resolution strategy, individuals or groups try to reach an agreement that satisfies both their own and the other party's interests and goals. Instead of being adversarial, individuals take a team approach, identify the problem, and use methods such as brainstorming to come up with a creative solution so that everyone becomes a winner.

Instead of attacking each other, they collectively attack the problem. Everyone openly indicates their real needs, and the group searches for a solution that will satisfy everyone. Although a collaborative approach takes time, and should not be used to solve every conflict, cohesion and high morale are the benefits.

Each of these strategies is useful under certain circumstances, in handling both interpersonal and departmental conflict. However, the approach that creates a win-win situation is collaboration. In most cases, the problem is solved, and the relationship between the parties is maintained or becomes even better because both individuals have been listened to and treated with respect. Using active listening, or paraphrasing what the other party is saying, lets that party know that you hear and understand his or her position.

It is important that you know that there is more than one approach in handling conflict and that any of them may be the method of choice in a particular circumstance. The saying "When the only tool you have is a hammer, every problem will be treated like a nail" indicates that when you have only one option for handling a problem and you use the same approach for all situations, a poor outcome is guaranteed. The goal in conflict management is to be aware of all the strategies available, the pros and cons of each one, and to select the approach that is likely to work best in a particular situation. When handling conflict in a group, it is also helpful to know that conflict can be expected at different points in the life of a group.

STAGES OF GROUP DEVELOPMENT IN A DEPARTMENT

From the time that they form, all groups pass through predictable stages, including one that is rampant with conflict, before they become a smoothly functioning group. When an individual assumes the role of head of a department or director of a unit, a new group is formed that must go through at least a shortened version of the stages all groups pass through before becoming fully effective as a team. This is true even when a department has been made up of the same staff members for years. These stages of group development, first mentioned by Bruce W. Tuchman in the mid-1960s, are *forming, storming, norming,* and *performing.*

Forming

When an administrator is appointed, a new group *forms,* and members begin to redefine their goals and develop procedures for performing their tasks. Since individuals don't know whether having the new leader will change the way they have been doing things, they often keep feelings to themselves until they know what to expect, are often unusually polite to one another, and are tentative in their relationships as they test the water. This may well be what is often referred to as the leader's "honeymoon" period.

Storming

At the second stage, *storming,* friction arises over how tasks should be performed and by whom. Authority, leadership, decision making, and how conflicts are handled are all questioned. Procedures for functioning together are dealt with, often indirectly, sometimes abrasively. Members of the department may be concerned about how much change the new leader is going to put in place, and whether she or he will exercise more control than the previous leader. For example, in one department a former head never wrote a memo, and all information was conveyed to the members orally through the secretary. The new department head, wanting to use a more direct channel for keeping people informed, wrote memos about relevant issues and placed these in individuals' mailboxes. This resulted in complaints about getting too many memos from the administrator, and department members recommended that all notices be placed on a bulletin board instead of in individuals' mailboxes. The administrator agreed and used the procedure department members recommended. However, when several people missed a meeting they wanted to attend because they had forgotten to look at the bulletin board where the change in time had been posted, they displaced their anger on the department head for not notifying them personally about the change in the time for the meeting. Much of the conflict at this second stage has an element of irrationality about it. Conflicts about leadership and goals are dominant themes. Some people may withdraw and isolate themselves from the stress and tension that result. In one department, the leader discontinued department meetings because they were stressful. Instead, he and his cronies made decisions over lunch in his office where they regularly met on Wednesdays at noon. This strategy included both the use of power and avoidance of conflict. The key role that an effective administrator plays during this stage is to manage the conflict, not suppress it or withdraw from it.

Norming

In the third stage, *norming,* the group collects and shares information, accepts different points of view, develops the rules by which they will solve problems and make decisions, and, if all goes well, begins to develop cohesion. Cooperation, humor, and positive expressions of feeling toward one another predominate. But this is also the time when individuals establish dysfunctional behaviors if they are accepted (reinforced) by the group. For example, in one department two individuals continually arrived late for meetings and then demanded that any decisions made by the group before their arrival be voted upon again if the latecomers disagreed with the action taken. When the administrator and the group permitted such conduct rather than confront it as dysfunctional behavior, they reinforced unacceptable actions that continued unabated at future meetings.

Performing

At the final stage, *performing,* the group becomes an effective, cohesive group of individuals who perform their functions well. Individuals become aware of each member's strengths and begin to operate on the basis of rules that were determined at stage three. When there is clarification of such issues as who will take which roles, what procedures will be used, how problems will be resolved, and how decisions will be made, the group can function well. The role of the administrator, throughout these stages, is to help define the task of the group, place it in a positive framework, create a smooth link with the individual to whom the group reports, and work on creating effective interpersonal relationships in the department. Defining the task of the group often involves revisiting the department mission and policy statements so that people can agree on goals and implementation steps. This process will help get individual perspectives out in the open where they can be dealt with. The leader must also initiate difficult conversations and align different points of view so that everyone has an investment in the final documents. Allowing—or even encouraging—conflict, while not permitting personal attacks, creates a framework that shows department members that it is safe to disagree. Individuals can begin to appreciate that disagreement in the early part of a discussion can be useful in identifying the issues, so disagreements can be turned into problems to be solved instead of creating adversarial relations between people, which can fragment a department.

Dysfunctional Groups

Some groups never resolve the issues pertinent to stages two and three (storming and norming) and continue storming, tolerating dysfunctional behavior, and creating negative norms and rules that continue for the rest of the group's existence, or until those negative norms have been confronted and changed. If destructive conflict in a department has continued over a period of a year, and the best efforts of the leader seem insufficient to defuse a toxic environment, it often helps to bring in an outside process consultant to assist the department in working through their strife so they can better function together. Since groups frequently say, "We don't wash dirty linen in public," they may be reluctant to call in an outside consultant. The director, or the leader's supervisor, may have to intervene to assure them that all groups move through this series of stages and that their methods of handling conflict are a barrier to their accomplishing their goals. Somewhere along the line, they have learned some unsuccessful ways of handling conflict. These can be unlearned and replaced with more effective approaches. An outside consultant—perhaps someone from the human resources department—with the necessary skills can help them work through these difficulties.

STRATEGIES FOR PREVENTING AND RESOLVING SPECIFIC INTRAGROUP PROBLEMS

Diversity

As more department heads and staff retire, and more junior people take their place, academic administrators find a whole new collection of challenges, which may create serious conflict. More women, people of color, younger individuals, those with disabilities, and residents from abroad are joining higher education. Although such diversity brings a new set of resources and different perspectives, which can revitalize a department, they also bring change that requires adjustment on the part of administrators.

New employees and senior staff often start out with some negative preconceptions about each other, and a framework of complaints develops that can exacerbate interactions between them. Once again, the department head has a key role to play here and must do whatever can be done to create a level playing field, perhaps by asking senior staff to serve as mentors to newcomers, providing recognition to senior staff for excellent or innovative work, giving minority members opportunities to make specific contributions at meetings, using occasions to celebrate accomplishments, and encouraging informal social events so that individuals can get to know one another as human beings, not just in their designated roles in the department. One administrator of a newly diversified division encouraged individuals from different cultures to bring in a dish typical of food from their country to a potluck lunch held during the holiday season. At the end of this festive occasion, employees asked if such an event could be scheduled on a regular basis.

Difficult People

In many departments there are some individuals who are difficult colleagues. In some situations individuals have become curmudgeons because of negative thinking, which was addressed in Chapter Three. First, it is important to spend time thanking individuals for their contributions to the department and to the college or university. Although most individuals working in higher education feel undervalued, negative thinkers are particularly likely to feel unappreciated. A department head who sees individuals in the department every day is in an ideal position to show appreciation for what employees are doing. Immediate reinforcement is most effective, a comment that is appropriate to what has been done, not extravagant praise. Lavish comments often lose their power because they seem insincere. Another useful strategy is to help difficult colleagues to identify a problem as an issue to resolve, rather than as an obstacle they cannot surmount, and offer your help.

Sometimes dependent individuals will seek an enormous amount of your time. A director stated that one of her department heads came to see her at least once a day with a problem. When she solved it for him, he told her how intuitive she was, how much he appreciated her help, how his life would be miserable without her assistance, how grateful he was, and so forth. The director, of course, liked to hear this. So she was rewarding his seeking help on a daily basis, and he was making her feel that she was doing a good job as director. After she suggested that he come with at least two solutions to each problem and tell her the one he preferred most, his visits to her were cut significantly.

Inadequate Job Performance

Sometimes a director or department head confronts situations in which individuals' job performance is inadequate. They may continue in the job for years because the person in charge does not have the courage to fire them. The first approach would be to interview the employee to discover his or her perspective on what the problem seems to be. If there seem to be no specific barriers that can be removed, discuss what the desired performance is and look with the individual at the gap between what is expected and what he or she is doing. Set time lines for changed behavior and interview the individual again at that time. Confronting individuals with uncooperative behavior is a difficult task and is not something most supervisors enjoy doing. However, if all else fails and an employee does not behave in a collegial fashion and is abrasive or unwilling to do his or her share of the work, he or she can be fired with adequate documentation and feedback. In any case, documentation of observable behavior is essential. Therefore, a primary lesson is not to let things build up to where conflict is almost unmanageable, but based on observable behavior, to confront individuals whose performance is unacceptable, to identify the problem to be solved, and together with the individual, to generate alternative ways of behaving.

Search and Screen Committees

Although some friction is the result of a long build-up of discord that has been ignored or allowed to fester, some conflict may be created by the way policy and procedures are used in a department. High on this list is the manner in which search and screen committees are handled. When Sam Adiamo retired, a search and screen committee was set up to recommend a new director of library services. After considerable deliberation, all but one member of the committee, Robert, voted to select John Jefferson to take Sam's place. After John had been appointed to the position, he announced to the staff that he was going to transform the library. He changed people's responsibilities, combining work from different units that had not been linked together before. When he announced these changes at a staff meeting, people generally seemed to accept what John had done, with the exception of Robert, who had been stripped of many responsibilities. Robert said that he felt that a game of musical chairs was being played, and he was the one left standing.

Without knowing more about this incident, it is impossible to draw conclusions about the motivation and perceptions of each of the people involved. However, on the surface, it does seem as if more than chance factors are operating in Robert's being stripped of his major responsibilities after voting against the appointment of John Jefferson. This serves as a reminder of the casualties that frequently occur when confidentiality is broken by members of search and screen committees. We have observed many such incidents with serious consequences over the course of our work in higher education. One excellent way to prevent this is to have someone at a higher administrative level convene the committee, thank them for undertaking this important work, perhaps present them with a job description of the position they will be helping to fill, inform them of the procedure, for example, submitting at least three names in order of preference, inform them of the gravity of their responsibilities, and advise them of the harm that can be done to other members of the committee if confidentiality is broken.

HANDLING CONFLICT AT DEPARTMENT MEETINGS

When a department is troubled, conflict often manifests itself at department meetings. Members of the department may engage in frequent personal attacks on one another, or the conflict may go underground, surfacing only in seemingly rational objections to motions put forward by "the enemy." How the department head or director handles conflict at meetings will help determine whether adversarial relations will become worse or will be helped to heal. A leader may periodically use a meeting audit form to discover participant satisfaction and dissatisfaction with different aspects of the meeting. A meeting audit simply requires that members list two or three items that they liked about the meeting, two or three factors that they disliked, and two or three suggestions of how meetings could be improved. Each of the items listed is then rated on a continuum from 1 (a great deal of satisfaction) to 6 (relatively little satisfaction). Forms can be prepared in advance with copies that can be used at meetings as often as a chair feels it is worthwhile. At the following meeting, it is useful to share the results of the meeting's audit with participants and ask for their advice on changing those aspects of the meeting that people felt were unproductive. Notice that an administrator need not take complete responsibility for meetings that members of the department are unhappy about. If individuals have an opportunity for input and view having successful meetings as partially their obligation, planning and conducting effective meetings becomes everyone's assignment. It is a team function.

Another intervention that can be helpful in improving the effectiveness of meetings is called "stop action," a strategy for detaching ourselves from the content of a meeting to look at what is happening within the group. If the meeting seems to be going nowhere, or if individuals are making personal attacks instead of sticking with the issues, the department head, or another strong individual, simply calls, "stop action." Once an individual has done this, the next step is to ask people to disengage themselves from the meeting, share their observations about what is going on, and ask if that is what they want to be doing at this point in the meeting. An administrator needs to be patient with this intervention since members often have difficulty disengaging themselves from the content, particularly when emotions are high, and in the beginning, they may not be good observers of dynamics or process. The intervention may also be useful when group involvement is minimal. "Stop action" may be used as a tool to discover why many people are silent at a time when the topic is one the leader thought would engage everyone. Such interventions encourage openness and discussions about change that members would like to bring about.

Task and Relationship Roles in a Group

For a group to function effectively, both leader and members must pay attention to task and maintenance behaviors. Task behaviors achieve the goals for which the group is organized. Although the issues discussed at department meetings may change from month to month, they all deal with handling the concerns of the department. Maintenance behaviors, on the other hand, contribute to the group's being in good working order; they deal with the relationship aspects of small group dynamics, that is whether all individuals feel respected by the group, have a sense of inclusion, and feel free to express their opinions.

Unless a leader pays attention to the dynamics of group functioning—maintenance—attempts to achieve the task of the group get bogged down. Further, when decisions are reached without attention to maintenance roles, there will be little commitment to goals on the part of those who feel their opinions were not taken seriously. Therefore, these same individuals will be unwilling to work to implement decisions that were made or to accomplish the goals of the department. Since many leaders complain that they cannot get their department members to assume responsibility for the work of the department (which can be a source of conflict), they might look at the way decisions are made and goals are set to discover whether they have used a process of participative decision making to develop commitment. If some do not participate in discussions at meetings, their views need to be polled directly, and they need to be listened to. Until department members become skilled in small group dynamics, at which time all members are responsible for task and maintenance functions, an administrator may want to specifically assign to others some of the responsibility for meetings.

A leader can demonstrate interest in having productive meetings by asking two members to be accountable for task and maintenance functions. The job of the task leader is to record information on a flip chart, keep track of assignments, and prepare and circulate minutes. However, the task leader also assists participants by summarizing points of agreement, helps individuals decide what approach they will use to solve a problem, reminds them not to criticize during brainstorming, keeps people on the topic, and tries to get closure when there is little disagreement but people are talking a lot. The maintenance or relationship leader tries to keep abrasive members from alienating themselves from the group by paraphrasing what they have said, or asking them to explain or elaborate on a point they have made. In addition, the maintenance leader tries to ensure broad participation by bringing quiet members into the discussion. Since silence often means disagreement, rather than agreement, everyone needs to be given a chance to express an opinion. When members are silent, looking at them as another individual speaks, occasionally nodding or smiling, or calling upon them directly includes them and makes it easier for them to contribute. Getting silent members involved also minimizes their leaving a meeting feeling angry.

The task and relationship responsibilities can be given to members on a rotating basis from meeting to meeting. Such assignments will pique the interest of group members, and their reporting back to the group periodically throughout the meeting will also supply feedback to the rest of the participants on their role in discussions. Obviously this is an important time for the leader to ensure that the climate is supportive, with more positive than negative feedback furnished.

The way in which meetings are conducted, turning conflicts into problems to be solved, provides a model for handling conflicts between members at other times. Paraphrasing what people have said supports their right to express themselves and affirms feelings of being accepted in the group. A sense of humor helps. Enlisting the aid of other influential members of the department before meetings is very useful. The important thing is to be aware that you are not alone in the trenches with complete responsibility for making things go well. If the work of the department is a team effort, you will have all the help that you need.

Preventing and Healing Rifts in Groups

A potential rift in a group can also be handled by giving an empathic response that affirms the value of an angry person and helps him or her to calm down. For example, an angry, red-faced individual arrived fifteen minutes late for an important committee meeting. He entered the room stating, "I drove around the parking lot for twenty minutes, unable to find a parking space. Unless I am given an assigned space, I will resign from this committee." The chair of the committee responded, "I can understand your frustration. There just aren't enough parking spaces. But you contribute so much to this committee's work, we really need you." Somewhat mollified, the individual sat down and in a few minutes began to participate in the discussion. Without this supportive statement of being valued, the individual in the heat of anger might have gone ahead and resigned. Although it may seem as if adults don't need to have their feathers smoothed, once they take an action (such as resignation from a committee), they will often identify a list of grievances that justifies their lack of participation, and we have lost their commitment to future activities.

In a team-building workshop in a large department, a problem was uncovered in which one person had not allowed himself to be engaged in any departmental discussion for years because he believed the rest of the department members had not taken seriously some advice he had given them. At a department meeting four years before, he had made a statement that their body language showed anger and defensiveness, so they needed to talk about their emotions before addressing the content of a particular topic. There was a moment or two of silence, after which the rest of the department members simply went on with their discussion. He felt that they were ignoring him and his valuable advice. He thought, "If they don't feel my opinion is worth anything, I just won't offer it anymore." So, instead of simply ignoring the possibility that someone has been hurt, we need to observe and be concerned about the reactions and behavior of people in the department to be certain that they have not been offended. Otherwise we will lose the talents and contributions all members of a department can provide. After all, when the department hired this person, we thought he had something valuable to offer. Somehow a barrier was erected that stopped the flow of those contributions. We need to help the individual tear down the barrier and build a bridge with others in the department. Affirming for the individual the value he brings to the department is a good beginning.

As we discussed in Chapter One, conflict is not, in and of itself, destructive. It can be used creatively to broaden our understanding, increase our options, and generate a high energy level that can increase participation and commitment to a group decision. Constructive conflict allows department members to cooperate and support one another's ideas. Individuals become open to considering the merits of opinions different from their own. Disagreements are limited to issues and do not involve attacks on personalities. Members of the department understand the usefulness of conflict and manage it effectively. They assume disagreements stem from sincere involvement and that discussing different ideas will result in a better solution.

In disruptive conflict, the climate is competitive; a win-lose situation is created. Individuals become convinced that they are right and look for reasons that will bolster their positions, rather than being receptive to information that might support their opponents' ideas. Enlisting others in their personal cause becomes more important than finding the best solution for the group's problem.

SUMMARY

A discussion of the major strategies for managing conflict, when they work and when they don't, provides an array of choices for academic leaders who must prevent conflict from disrupting a department. Knowing the stages of group development, and how and when to intervene, offers hope for those who feel that their group must be permanently dysfunctional because they can't resolve conflict. The strategies for preventing and resolving specific problems, including dealing effectively with difficult situations, handling inadequate performance, preventing toxic consequences of conflict related to the work of search and screen committees, and handling conflict at department meetings, equips academic administrators with effective approaches to untangling serious conflicts. Information on negative thinking reframes some of these problems. Finally, understanding the task and relationship aspects of small group dynamics provides interventions that not only can be used for conflict resolution in the department but also serve as a model for departmental committees.

6

Intergroup Conflict

Conflict on a Larger Scale

ONE OF THE CHALLENGES of working with conflict is that our knowledge from theory, research, and practice covers such broad areas and disciplines—the micro levels of individual behavior in psychology and social psychology to the macro political and social structures to the global influences of political science and international relations—that few have successfully integrated it all. Much of the research is on the psychology of people in conflict or on the predictability of people's behavior. Too little has focused on the interaction or dynamics of conflict, which is pertinent to understanding intergroup conflict.

In many ways the patterns and processes we discussed at each level—intrapersonal, interpersonal, and intragroup—are mirrored or have similarities when we consider intergroup conflict, or conflict between groups. At the intrapersonal level, excessive and unmanaged conflict within ourselves may impair our ability to fully understand the importance or complexity of the larger context within which we are struggling. As with interpersonal conflicts, we probably have needs and wants that interfere with the group's achieving its goals. Intragroup conflict reflects ways we think about others within the group. What is particularly unique to intergroup conflict, though, is the high degree of competitiveness that emerges between groups. Although poorly managed conflicts at all levels will heighten animosity and diminish morale, the unique nature of intergroup conflicts—conflict between groups whereby the interaction of the individuals is influenced by their group identification—can be especially troublesome.

CONFLICT BETWEEN GROUPS IN THE ACADEMY

In higher education, intergroup conflict has historical roots. Students often complain about poor teaching and grading. Faculty often talk about poor academic preparation of entering students: they cannot write well enough, have insufficient critical thinking skills, are not fully committed to their studies because of work schedules, or invest too much time in social activities. Staff and faculty believe that athletic programs inappropriately drain resources from the academic endeavor. They also complain about having too many administrators spending too much money on office furniture or travel at a time when their own salaries are low.

Competition among groups over scarce resources is played out when one group gets the resources at the other's expense. This is most apparent during budget deliberations. Most budgeting decisions are made by senior administrators, so predictably middle-level staff and faculty complain that these administrators have greater access to power and information, and are better able to influence decision making. Most people want to be members of the group that has the resources instead of the group that does not. Therefore, groups have similar goals: get what we want and prevent the other from getting what they want, which can result in highly aggressive behavior with little concern for the rights of the other group. In other words, the sources of intergroup conflict tend to be competitive in nature, perhaps over scarce resources, or are responses to what is perceived as inappropriate and adversarial behavior of the other. Intergroup conflict escalates as various constituency groups—students, staff, faculty, administrators—emerge as identity groups whereby the membership in the respective group is escalated in importance.

SOCIAL INFLUENCE OF GROUPS

In addition to the competitive nature of intergroup conflict, we cannot ignore ways that groups influence individual behavior. Social influence involves the process by which the group can change the feelings, thoughts, or behaviors of its individual members. When alone, we are freer to act as we want. Groups influence us by limiting our options and encouraging us to *conform,* sometimes resulting in redefining our perspective and shaping our understanding of situations. This is especially common when individual thinking varies too greatly from the thinking of the group.

The power of group conformity has been well documented—the 1930s study of social norms by Mazafer Sherif and the 1950s work of Solomon Asch as two of the most famous—and we know that individuals can and will significantly change their behavior because of group pressure and group identity. Whether subjects of conformity research experiments think the group must be right and they are wrong (when confronted with what seems to be an obviously wrong answer), or they do not want to be thought of as "odd" by members of the group, or they believe the other members may be going along to support one another, subjects are consistently influenced by the group behavior and, in most cases, conform to it.

Individuals also turn to groups for confirmation. Stanley Schachter's studies in the 1950s on affiliation demonstrated the need to compare and align our personal viewpoints with the views expressed by others in the group to assure ourselves of being correct. This seems especially important under conditions of high anxiety.

Much research by social psychologists since the 1950s has tried to understand the dynamics of conformity and nonconformity. We know that when individuals change their publicly stated position to agree with group opinion, they do so because they have either *converted* their private position to the group opinion (as did Asch's subjects) or *complied* with the group position (just going along). In cases when people refuse to go along with group opinion, they do so because of their *independence*— standing strong on their own beliefs—or because of *anticonformity,* where even if they agree privately with the group, they will take the opposite position publicly.

Why is this research important? It helps explain how members of a group become more cohesive when they form an adversarial position toward another group. Conformity and compliance are present in most intergroup conflicts. The interactive effects of the sources of intergroup conflict—competition, categorization (distinguishing characteristics of one group versus another such as race, gender, political party affiliation, or position), and identity (how a group defines itself)—and the resulting belligerent influence patterns, make the complexity of intergroup conflict especially interesting. A case is useful here.

BEGINNINGS OF INTERGROUP CONFLICT: COMPETITION

The administrative staff at a private university were unhappy about two issues: (1) the salary scale, which was significantly lower than scales at similar colleges and universities in the region, and (2) the working conditions, which required periodic weekend and evening hours. Staff were not able to get these concerns addressed to their satisfaction, and as a result many believed that it was necessary for them to organize. In the midst of this quiet grumbling, a long-time and admired member of the staff invited a union executive board member from a nearby university to speak to the staff about the value of being represented by a union. The speech generated a great deal of enthusiasm for unionization.

This is the beginning of an intergroup conflict. There appear to be limited resources and one group—management—holds decision-making power at the perceived expense of the other group—staff. First, a decision had to be made about whether or not staff would join a union. Second, if they decided to unionize, how would they proceed? Most staff agreed—either by conformity or compliance—that they should unionize. However, there was significant disagreement as to the priorities of concerns regarding salary and working conditions. Some wanted to focus only on salary to maximize the likelihood of getting significant raises. Others were most concerned about reclaiming their evenings and weekends.

The college was under financial pressure to increase programmatic offerings. The provost developed two initiatives: a robust evening and weekend undergraduate degree-completion program, and a partial residential distance-learning program. Each administrative office was required to configure its staffing to cover evenings, weekends, and the four two-week residentials over the academic year. No longer did staff work from 8:30 A.M. to 5:00 P.M. Monday through Friday.

Escalation

The staff became fragmented, and two subgroups formed around those wanting increased salaries and those wanting greater control of their work schedule. (A third group remained opposed to unionization and was systematically ignored by the other two.) As groups began to coalesce, conflict escalated. The groups quickly became identified as "us" and "them." Informally, staff from each group visited some of the offices of staff aligned with the other group trying to influence them to switch. These representatives spread negative stories about the other group. The original issues of salary scales and working conditions were preempted by character assassinations of members of the "other group."

What can we predict will happen? Each group wanted its issues to be the primary focus if represented by a union. Though the greater intergroup conflict (management versus staff) escalated, the intragroup conflict about salary and working conditions prevailed. The staff invited the National Labor Relations Board to conduct an election. There ultimately was strong support (more than 80 percent) to unionize. Though two groups of staff formed, they were now represented by one union. Immediately the relationship between staff and senior administration became more adversarial, and the intragroup conflict subsided. The newly unionized staff made demands for both salary increases and greater control over working conditions. Management refused on the grounds that they could not afford to raise salaries, and the university needed additional programmatic offerings to attract more students.

Why did the two adversarial groups of staff unite? Based on the conformity research, the staff engaged in either conversion or compliance. Some changed their position to the group's position, seemingly not wanting to be out of step with the others. Some disagreed privately but publicly complied. They believed management had greater power and influence, and there needed to be a larger collective to have staff voices recognized.

The conflict escalated when management refused to increase salaries. Staff went on strike one week after the beginning of the semester. A few days after the strike began, staff went to their mail boxes to pick up their salary checks and were quite surprised to discover that there were none. "How could management do this to us? It just proves they are as ill-intentioned as we thought they were."

Clearly the intergroup (staff versus senior administration) competition was now very strong. Intergroup competition parallels intragroup (within a group) competition with one important exception. It is more powerful, because group competition tends to be stronger than individual competition. We will return to the complexities of our case shortly.

Identity and Categorization

This brings us to the second source of conflict between groups: issues of identity and categorization. One of our basic human needs is identity. We often make sense of our environment by classifying it into categories that include groups to whom we belong and groups to whom we do not belong. Beginning in early childhood we learn to define ourselves— our identity—in terms of social groups: I am an Oregonian; I am a New Englander; I am a Methodist; or I am an Eagle Scout. This also includes groups to whom we do not belong: I am not a Southerner; I am not a Catholic; I am not a Democrat; I am not a jock. As soon as we learn categorization, we develop ways to describe people within the categories. The definitions vary depending on who is making the categorization. Staff descriptions of the category of management will be different than management's descriptions of the same category. By the time we are employed in higher education, we comfortably think of ourselves as classified but not exempt staff; tenured (or tenure-track) faculty but not contract or adjunct faculty; administrators but not faculty; management but not union; and so on.

Classification systems, at the most basic level, become "us" versus "them." You are a member of my group, or you are a member of the other group. Returning to our case, the staff appear, on the surface, as one group. But the complexity of their interests and values demonstrates that, in fact, they have very different opinions about what priorities should prevail. These differences result in escalated conflict between groups of staff. This phenomenon is known as group differentiation. Differentiation reflects a polarization between groups, often accompanied by stereotyping of the "other." Stereotypes usually reflect highly simplified beliefs about characteristics of the other. Needless to say, this can ignite conflict. Taken to an extreme, we can develop intergroup ideologies that give us permission to say the other group is bad and we are good, or at least to explain why.

Staff realized that divided they could not get support for either of their concerns. It was under these conditions that categorization returned: staff versus senior administration (management). Categorization is also strongly connected to social identity. Employees, students, and alumni form beliefs about themselves ("good guys") and the others ("bad guys"). Their individual identity is defined in part by their being a member of a successful group. They must work to maintain and protect this social identity, and therefore will enhance it by finding evidence of their own superiority and the inferiority of the others. This sustains their willingness to engage in contentious and competitive behaviors. At the same time, an interesting phenomenon occurs. There is a significant increase in group cohesion and clearer distinction of the boundaries and identity of the conflicting groups. In our case, boundaries between the staff and senior administrative groups were reinforced when staff went on strike and management refused to pay them. Rather than see their similarities—all part of a larger university system—they differentiated themselves from each other. Interestingly, this occurred with both groups. The staff declared they now had proof that management was every bit as ill-intentioned as they had originally believed. Management declared that the staff were self-absorbed and unwilling to work for the good of the university.

Once these kinds of categories emerge, members acquire in-group and out-group bias. Campus personnel favor their own group and make derogatory remarks about the other. Group pressure to conform also escalates. This was best illustrated when staff lobbied individuals to join their special interest group.

Belligerent and competitive behaviors often result in insults, humiliation, threats, and intimidation. Relatively minor disagreements can spiral into full-fledged and large-scale conflicts. (We have all witnessed, at least through the news, race riots or wars between countries caused by escalating hostile exchanges.) Yet research also demonstrates that in-group cohesion and feelings of superiority are stronger than out-group rejection. This occurs because feeling better than the other group reinforces high morale and strong group cohesion. With such positive group identity, members exhibit high self-esteem. Just as important, research informs us that our expressions of hostility tend to be situational. Hostility can be lessened depending on the similarities of the two groups such as their membership, anticipated future interactions, and the cooperative versus competitive nature of their intergroup situation.

It is problematic to think that intergroup conflict is primarily due to intergroup *differences.* If this were true, conflict would be inevitable between any groups that are different. The mere fact that the groups have particular characteristics—all men, all women, all administrators, or faculty and administrators in one college versus those of another—would move these groups to be obvious enemies. How do we explain, then, other people with similar characteristics that are not part of the conflict? It is much more useful to consider the intergroup *interaction* when we try to understand the conflict. While the differences may contribute to the intensity and sustainability of the conflict, the conflict exists primarily because of our prejudices about these differences. If we believe that the other group is bad or wrong or getting in our way, or is unevenly receiving limited available resources, then we identify individuals as members of a group and describe the group as hostile and conflictually dissonant.

BEYOND ANALYSIS: RESOLUTION OF INTERGROUP CONFLICT

It seems much easier to analyze why conflict between groups escalates than to sort out what to do about it. Methods of handling such conflicts are further explained in Chapter Seven on interventions. Nevertheless, this is a good time to reintroduce our framework found in Figure 2.1 (on page 14).

Knowledge of the social science research increases our understanding and analysis of a conflict and ultimately informs our choices of possible solutions. Returning to our case, several *situational* (Level II) and *structural* (Level III) factors could be used as part of an intervention by staff and administrative leaders. The situation was ripe for unionization because of a perceived win-lose model on campus. Staff thought they were underpaid, and administrators reassigned their working hours to "cover" new academic programs.

When groups complain of injustices it signals the academic administrator that something is awry. Regardless of whether or not there are limited resources, or that it will be necessary to cover evening and weekend classes, these are excellent opportunities for groups to work together. A salary and benefit task force could be created, representing both staff and administration. This task force could be *facilitated* by the administrator or one of the group members (chair), who is charged with collecting pertinent data—actual salaries at similar colleges within the region—and developing collaboratively based recommendations about how to address the concerns. It might result in a phased-in plan for salary increases over several years.

Similarly, if the hours of operation are significantly changed, a group could be formed of staff and senior administrators to study the situation. They too could be charged with creating recommendations that would address the problem. Task forces become *structures* (Level III) that allow groups to work collaboratively. When these groups perceive opportunities to problem-solve, parties are more likely to feel they can contribute to finding a fair and equitable solution.

One outcome of common problem solving is that the differences between groups—responsibilities, values, perspectives, and so on—are utilized so that these differences become assets rather than irritants. It also helps parties realize their similarities are often greater than their differences.

SUMMARY

Though colleges and universities are not immune to intergroup conflict, we acknowledge the special and useful nature of the academy's espoused cultural values (Level III) in both preventing and resolving some inter-group conflict. We know that as intergroup conflict escalates, stereotypes, bias, and ethnocentrism increase. For the most part, members of colleges and universities reject these categorizations. Stereotyping the out-group is too simplistic, monolithic, and extreme a behavior. The other group becomes more homogeneous than our own group, and we make claims about that group based on little data and too few members. Staff seldom like to be thought of as a singular group. The same is true of adminis-trators. Therefore, demonstrating how our differences, capacities for crit-ical thinking, values of collaboration, and commitment to democratic processes can contribute to forming effective communities is likely to help members appreciate the liabilities of inappropriate categorization of the others and help change our own behavior. This might require a *facil-itated* diversity training, addressing Level II and III aspects of the conflict: the influence and interactive effects of situations, identities, culture, tra-ditions, and structures of our institutions including what is and is not working.

7

Conflict Intervention

ONFLICT INTERVENTION IS the part of conflict resolution that involves the various ways we try to cope with, manage, or resolve social conflicts. What strategies are available to you when two or more parties are expressing their differences in hostile ways? First, you need to learn as much as you can about the comprehensive nature of the conflict and its unique complexities. When you have a good understanding of the conflict you are better prepared to design an intervention.

In the academy there are a number of commonly used intervention strategies for serious conflicts, such as traditional models of facilitation, negotiation, mediation, and arbitration. Legal counsel, human resources, ombuds personnel, and counseling services are also available You can perform some of these strategies in your role as an administrator; for others you will need an outsider or third party to help. Administrators can be excellent interveners both because of the formal nature of your roles, and because you are likely to have already acquired many of the requisite skills in order to be effective doing your jobs.

This chapter revisits our frameworks introduced in Chapter Two so that we can best connect our conflict analysis (using Figure 2.1 on page 14) with a viable intervention strategy. It is important that the right "fit" exists between what we think is the problem and what we propose as the intervention.

Our diagnosis should involve the types, sources, and dynamics of the conflict (consider Level I questions); any identity or situational aspects pertinent to the conflict (Level II questions); and all aspects of the conflict embedded in the culture, traditions, and structures of the college or university (Level III questions). These were discussed in Chapters One and Two and consider the conflict from the micro through the macro levels. You may conclude that the primary issues of the conflict deal with power and authority, or poor morale and lack of cohesion, or differences in vision and mission, or lack of resources—all common examples.

Next, we look at the organizational location of involvement discussed in Chapters Three through Six. Is the conflict predominately intra-individual, interpersonal, intragroup, or intergroup? We may conclude that a conflict is interpersonal between a supervisor and a staff member, and the source of the conflict is an abuse of position power. Or, the conflict may involve multiple department heads—intergroup conflict—vying for limited resources due to mandated cutbacks.

Finally, and the focus of this chapter, we consider interventions appropriate for our diagnosis of the conflict. Here we ask such questions as: What strategies are most appropriate for an interpersonal conflict that has as its core differences in power and authority? Or what strategies can we consider when working with unit heads in the creation of an overall budget? The needs and issues are different, and therefore the strategies will vary. It is important to recognize that there may be several intervention possibilities, so it is necessary to evaluate the pros and cons of each one to determine what is likely to be the most workable and durable intervention.

Let us imagine that you are now facing a very difficult conflict. You have conducted a thorough analysis of the conflict in order to understand its predominant location (Levels I, II, or III in Figure 2.1). This is the first indicator of how to proceed. Conflicts are nearly always embedded: although the primary location may be at one level, issues at other levels will be reflected. Nevertheless, the primary location is an excellent starting point for conflict intervention. If your analysis suggests that it is a long-time interpersonal conflict (Level I), then you must consider an interpersonal intervention such as a mediation between the two parties. If, for example, the conflict tends to be identity-based (Level II), you need to develop some kind of intervention that focuses primarily on identity-based conflicts, such as a facilitated training demonstrating the usefulness of individual differences. Or, if the conflict focuses on the need to change the rules or culture (Level III), then some kind of structural intervention needs to occur that might include a problem-focused task force.

THE ADMINISTRATOR AS INTERVENER

There are a number of traditional intervention strategies that can be conducted by you as the academic administrator. Figure 7.1 introduces three interventions that are included in the boxes to the right. The first two boxes reflect traditional conflict resolution models: facilitation and negotiation—most easily adapted for use by the academic administrator—and mediation and arbitration—more likely used by a *neutral party*. The third box includes other specialized parties employed by the college or university such as the ombuds office, human resources, legal counsel, and specialized counseling services.

The lines intersecting the concentric circles in Figure 7.1 imply that our analysis of the conflict at each of the three levels should inform any decisions we make about strategies to manage or resolve the conflict. Facilitation and negotiation do not necessarily need a third party to conduct the intervention. In the larger field of conflict resolution, third parties are supposed to be *neutral,* without bias toward a particular outcome. However, in organizational conflict resolution—including conflicts in the academy—this is seldom the case. Supervisors, administrators, and leaders are supposed to be committed to resolution of departmental conflicts. While supervisors are sometimes part of the problem, they have as one of their responsibilities a commitment to "fix" the problem. Position power (the authority that comes with the job) needs to be used judiciously as it is both an asset—increasing the motivation of parties to address the conflict—and a liability—forcing parties to do what they may not want to do, and therefore not likely to produce an enduring settlement. So what do we mean by these intervention models? What follows is a brief background and discussion of traditional models of each. (Additional resources are suggested in the Recommended Reading section).

Figure 7.1. A Framework for Conflict Intervention

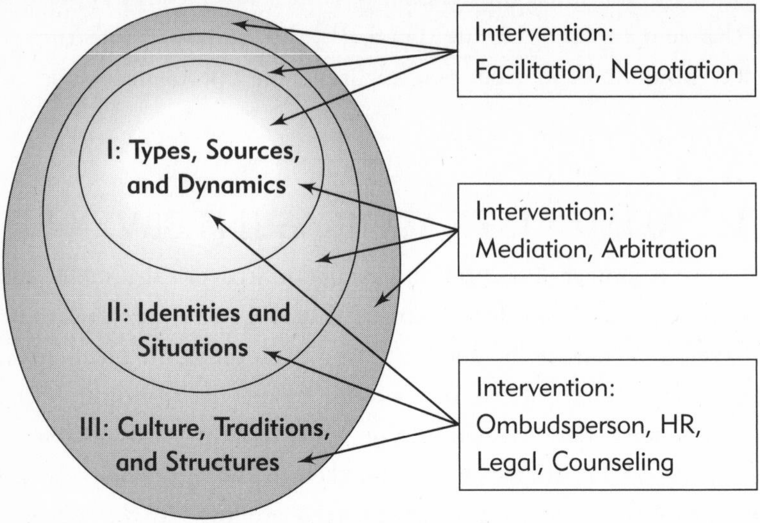

Source: Adapted from Cheldelin, Druckman, and Fast (2003).

FACILITATION

Much of the early research on and practice of facilitation occurred in England at the Tavistock Institute of Human Relations in London, and in the United States at the NTL Institute for Applied Behavioral Science (formally known as the National Training Laboratories) and the Gestalt Institute of Cleveland. In the early 1940s at Tavistock, researchers studied small groups and concluded that individuals' behavior could not be understood outside of the groups in which they live. Around the same time, Kurt Lewin and his colleagues studied identity-based conflicts and found that identity issues were a significant contributor to hostilities between groups. This became the foundation of the practice of group facilitation. In the 1950s psychologists at the Cleveland Institute began to provide training programs to teach facilitation skills needed for small and large groups—from families to large corporations.

Facilitation is conducted by a third party—usually an individual external to the conflict—whose task is to help disputants reach an agreement. In the conflict resolution literature, facilitation is often called an "assisted negotiation." Unlike mediation practices, which are usually between two parties, facilitation is used for multiparty meetings and consensus-building processes. The emphasis is on the negotiation *process* and less on the *substance* of the outcomes.

The typical steps in the process are as follows:

1. Conduct initial meetings—usually separate—with all parties involved in the conflict to clarify issues and goals

2. Obtain agreement on expectations, roles, and values

3. Convene a meeting where the facilitator (administrator) reviews the goals, creates ground rules, and presents informed reflections on the current situation

4. Help the group work on its task (to solve their problems, or create new visions, or identify obstacles to working collaboratively)

5. Conclude with an action plan and assignments for participants

6. Provide summary remarks

The facilitator is often considered a *guardian* of the process, encouraging and supporting participants in resolving their issues. This requires a number of group process skills: ensuring all members have an equal opportunity to speak and to be heard; clarifying goals and agendas; keeping the group focused; helping them accomplish their tasks; and "walking the talk" in terms of demonstrating capacities to listen, paraphrase, reframe, and otherwise model nonconflictual ways of working together.

Two of the models of facilitation that are particularly useful for academic administrators are to help the group problem-solve or to help the group generate a new image of their collective future. Problem solving, the most common, has an obvious "felt need," and parties come together to settle their differences. It involves articulating the problems, analyzing the causes, creating possible solutions, and developing a plan to move ahead. An alternative model—the most common is called appreciative inquiry—focuses on valuing what the collective group can do and envisioning where members of the group want to go. The two models need not be exclusive. The first facilitation meeting could focus on articulating the problems and working out ways to resolve them. Envisioning a different way of doing business together is a viable strategy to conclude a facilitation where people take into consideration all parties' hopes, desires, and goals, and create new strategies for working collaboratively.

Facilitation is an excellent strategy for large intra- or intergroup problems. An academic administrator may have the requisite skills to work with large groups but might be well served to ask a neutral third party to convene a consultation process that follows steps similar to small group facilitation. The goals of third-party facilitators are to problem-solve through improved communication and to analyze the basic relationship between the parties in conflict. Facilitation differs from mediation as it focuses on *process and analysis* rather than on substantive issues or specific *settlements.* Large group facilitations are generally organized as facilitated small group discussions. If the groups are so large that representatives are required, participants must be carefully selected. The facilitators should take into account the representatives' connections to important policy makers, opinion leaders, or influential members of their respective groups, as decisions and action plans resulting from the facilitation will ultimately need "buy-in" from the larger groups they represent.

NEGOTIATION

There are a number of popular definitions of negotiation in the field of conflict resolution. What they have in common is their focus on the importance of the relationship between process and outcome. Negotiation is an attempt to find some settlement by a process of giving and taking. Some kind of transaction goes on between the parties in all negotiations.

Consider the following situation. Your new employee, Joan, started work in your department three months ago. A critical report is due to your supervisor at the end of the week. You delegated a significant section of the report to be completed by Joan, which is due today. You were confident she knew how to do the task and had sufficient time to complete it. Joan came to you this morning, apologetically, informing you she does not have the report completed. Joan was concerned that she do an excellent job, so she decided to write the report in the evenings and on the weekends at home where she would be less distracted. Two days ago her home computer crashed, and she lost all of the nearly completed report. She had neglected to back-up her file. You are furious as your own reputation is on the line. How could she be so careless? What are you going to do now?

This conflict is ripe for negotiation by you even though you are one of the parties involved. By definition, negotiation focuses on the relationship between process and outcome. You *attempt to settle* how you can get the report completed on time. Each of you *shall give and take*, or *perform and receive* in a *transaction* between you. This means you and Joan will have to come to a mutual agreement about what will happen. You may fire her, but that is outside the realm of negotiation and does not resolve your problem of getting the report to your supervisor by the end of the week. There are other possible negotiation alternatives, however. You may ask her to stay home to complete the report, putting all other work responsibilities on hold. (This allows her to demonstrate that she can do the work and prevents delays caused by typical work-day distractions.) You may ask her to complete her other work assignments on the weekend. (This allows you to make her responsible for her misbehavior.) In a negotiation you are faced with making a decision that is acceptable to both you and Joan. Negotiation presumes that each of you wants to engage in the conflict—not avoid it—and therefore is willing to address the other's needs and concerns. A compromise is likely to be the outcome.

There is extensive research on negotiation, but we are most interested in the processes that directly apply to when you, as the administrator, are involved in the conflict. Four approaches seem most pertinent. These are negotiations primarily based on power, interests, rights, or transformation.

Power-based negotiations require interpersonal power—the capacity of individuals to influence one another—and an interest in winning at all costs. These negotiations are competitive, with the goal to maximize personal gain. Resolution is usually based on the strongest party: who has the most political clout or access to the largest amount of resources, or is the most intelligent. Administrators too often use this type of negotiation with subordinates because of their position power. Though power-based negotiations may settle an immediate conflict, subordinates are likely to keep score and take revenge when the opportunity presents itself. It undermines morale and departmental cohesiveness, and ultimately leads to poorer performance.

Interest-based negotiations have goals of moving parties away from adversarial *positions* toward addressing the parties' *underlying interests.* What do the parties really want to achieve? Consider this case of a new registrar, Adrian, the department chair, Jim, and a member of the chair's faculty, Susan. It highlights a successful multiparty interest-based negotiation. This took place at a metropolitan university where most of the classes began at 4:30 P.M. Adrian, trying to understand the needs of the various academic departments, set up a meeting with the chair and his faculty to discuss class assignments in the context of limited classroom availability in the evenings. At the beginning of the meeting Susan blurted out: "I'm not going to teach the 7:30 evening classes on Tuesdays and Wednesdays. When I went to college, classes were scheduled beginning at 8:00 A.M., and went on throughout the day. If these students are serious about getting a college education, they can cut back on their work and come to class at a reasonable time. From now on I'm only going to offer my classes at 1:30." Susan then stomped out of the room. The other faculty snickered as they had experienced her rigidity in the past. Jim was embarrassed and irritated with the outburst and knew that he could use power-based negotiations, forcing her to teach at 7:30 P.M. Instead, after the meeting, he and Adrian met to try to determine what underlying needs caused Susan to take such a hard, seemingly irrational, position. Adrian reminded Jim that if Susan did teach at 1:30, it would help with the problem of too many courses scheduled for too few classrooms available in the evening.

They decided to meet with Susan separate from the rest of the faculty. Upon interviewing Susan they learned that she has five school-aged children in her new, blended family. It is difficult for her to teach in the evenings, but she does not want her personal life disclosed to members of the department. Coincidently, Jim has been considering starting a certificate program offering classes at work sites during the day (and Adrian is looking for relief from so many classes scheduled in the evenings). If Susan could teach in the certificate program, it would meet Susan's needs to teach during school hours, and the chair could launch the program bringing additional discretionary revenues to his department. Adrian has one less class to schedule. Everyone wins. Within the hour the parties came to an agreement about Susan taking the leadership in designing and implementing a new certificate program. Adrian agreed to find the best space on campus to schedule the new program (not in the evenings).

Rights-based negotiations focus on the legal aspects of the conflict. If parties know that public law would support one side of the conflict, then each is negotiating in what has been called "the shadow of the law." This is likely to influence both parties as they each know one party clearly has the upper hand should the conflict go to court. Rights-based negotiation extends beyond the law, however. It also considers the norms, rules, and traditions of the college. If you learn that one of your employees is an illegal immigrant and you decide to ignore this information, from a rights-based perspective you may expose the university to litigation. In most colleges, legal departments have recommended procedures to eliminate such a liability.

A case is useful here. Jesse, the new director of a small program, hired José, a handicapped applicant, knowing that he was unable to maneuver stairs. The program was temporarily housed in a building without elevators. Any office above the first floor was inaccessible. Jesse discussed the problem with José, and José decided that with the help of other staff, they could informally work out problems that might arise. Six months later, after successfully completing the probationary period, José presented a formal complaint to Jesse about not being able to fully participate as a member of the community because more than half of the office personnel were on the second floor. Jesse, defensive and feeling betrayed, reminded José of their informal agreement. José responded that at the time he was not able to fully understand the degree of jeopardy in which this would place him because he did not know enough about the social, cultural, and informal aspects of the program. He also noted that Jesse was too new to fully appreciate the unevenness of the deal Jesse offered. José requested that either an elevator be installed or the program be relocated to another building at the university that is handicapped accessible. Using a rights-based negotiation, José clearly had the legal system behind him. Rules, regulations, laws, customs, and traditions are all important to provide order and cooperation among members of any community. However, sole use of rights-based negotiation encourages parties to move to win-lose models: my rights supersede yours. When rights-based negotiations are initiated, informal strategies to resolve the conflict usually get sidelined by the legal system of attorneys or arbitrators, limiting creative possibilities for solutions that may work for all parties.

Transformation-based negotiations primarily focus on strategies that empower or recognize both parties. Empowering parties increases their sense of control and autonomy. Recognizing parties allows others to think and feel that they have been heard. Empowerment and recognition are important to obtain a collaborative outcome and improve any impairment in the relationship. Successful transformation negotiation processes allow parties to broaden their understanding of the perspectives of both parties, increase their capacities to consider options, improve their feelings about themselves and the other, and change their own behaviors to take into account the other's needs and interests. They improve empathy, listening, compassion, and other requisite skills to be effective conflict resolvers.

Returning to Susan, who needed to spend evenings with her family, Jim and Adrian were able to dislodge her from her belief that students should cut back on their work and her position that she would no longer teach in the evenings. As the conversation moved to greater options, Susan felt that her contributions were important (she would be designing and launching a new program) and her needs were real (she could rearrange her teaching schedule to spend more time with her family in the evenings). She also helped solve a university-wide problem of lack of available space during certain times of the day. Along with interest-based negotiations, Jim's skills of empowerment and recognition helped transform their relationship. Because transformation is designed to change people's behavior and their relationships, it requires a commitment to negotiations that takes time. It requires a capacity to understand the perspectives of the other and a willingness to provide a good faith effort of recognizing the worthiness of the other's concerns.

We now turn to two roles that are more formal than those used in facilitation or negotiation and are usually conducted by an outside third party: the mediator and the arbitrator. Mediation has a rich and varied history over centuries and across cultures. During the past few decades it has grown especially popular as a viable alternative to the legal system. Arbitration, though not as old (first recorded in the 1400s in England), dramatically increased in the 1940s during the growth of labor unions. Today, more than 95 percent of collective bargaining contracts provide for final and binding arbitration. Both are used often in higher education as an intervention method for conflict resolution.

MEDIATION

The Western model of mediation is the most commonly used model in colleges and universities. The process is confidential and voluntary and can be stopped at any time by any of the parties, including the mediator. It begins with the mediator making an initial assessment by interviewing each party. The mediator then convenes a meeting, establishes his or her role, outlines the process, sets ground rules, and creates structures for each party to state their perspectives about the dispute. The mediator then helps the parties achieve clarity on their issues, assists with collaborative problem solving, and concludes by drafting written agreements for parties to endorse and implement. Because mediators are supposed to be impartial—without a stake in the conflict—they are referred to as "neutral" and therefore do not impose decisions but rather serve as gatekeepers of a process.

This model of mediation is sometimes referred to as an extension or elaboration of the negotiation process. It uses an acceptable third party who has limited or no authoritative decision-making power. We can see immediately that most academic administrators would violate this premise should they conduct a mediation between their own employees whom they supervise. Nevertheless, many administrators successfully utilize mediation when both parties willingly come to the table.

Research consistently demonstrates the usefulness and practical outcomes of mediation. Mediation is less costly than court settlements, takes less time than courts to resolve conflicts, and has higher levels of compliance and lower relitigation rates. Mediation allows parties to express their wants, feelings, and concerns, and to discuss and work toward joint postagreement behavior without the time pressures of courts' calendars and without the financial pressures of high legal fees.

ARBITRATION

Arbitration is the settlement of a conflict by a person chosen to hear both sides and come to a decision. This is the broadest and most inclusive way of thinking about arbitration. It involves the selection of one or more neutrals who are experts or impartial third parties who hear the evidence and then make either binding or nonbinding decisions depending on the conditions of the arbitration. If binding, no follow-up litigation can occur. If nonbinding, the parties can chose to reenter the legal process.

Like mediation, arbitration is an alternative to litigation. It is less formal, usually less expensive, yet adversarial. It is most commonly used in the business arena, but it is not unusual to have arbitration a component of union contracts on campuses. Like mediation, arbitration is not without critics or problems. Only limited court review is permitted, and binding decisions cannot be appealed. Decisions often have little or no precedential value. Interestingly, though, there is some research that suggests that contrary to the conventional wisdom, arbitration may not be faster, cheaper, or fairer than a lawsuit, as the safeguards present in the courtroom are not available to parties in arbitration. Again, you must analyze the conflict and decide whether or not this is the appropriate strategy for intervention.

Hybrids

It is not entirely clear if the differences between arbitration and mediation make arbitration an advantage. Arbitrators retain control over the outcome. Thus, it is likely that little compromise can exist, which is often central to the outcomes of mediation. For this reason, the general practice in higher education includes some type of hybrid. The most popular hybrid is called *med-arb;* it combines the two processes of mediation and arbitration. Disputants select a neutral that will do both, allowing the intervener the benefit of problem solving, but ultimately giving him or her power to make a final decision.

Academic administrators have a history of creating their own intervention hybrids. A supervisor may bring the disputing parties to the table and offer them a process that is similar to formal mediation, with a clear understanding by all that if they cannot come to an agreement, the supervisor will decide and the parties will have to live with the decision. Joe and Mary were two staff members in a program who were consistently bickering with each other. For nearly two years, they undermined each other, created coalitions against each other, and otherwise made the work environment hostile. Shortly after the new program director was hired, he witnessed their behavior, interviewed others in the program, and then called Joe and Mary into his office. He offered them a formal mediation process that he would conduct. He said that the condition for the mediation was that if they could not work something out—and for the most part he did not care what the outcome looked like other than a willingness to change their behavior toward each other—he would initiate a process that could remove them from the program. Unlike traditional mediation, the director used his position power to impose a process that had serious consequences if the parties did not respond. Nevertheless, Joe and Mary agreed. They told their stories about the unpleasant conditions in which they worked, accused the other of misdeeds, and, with the assistance of the program director (in the role as mediator), developed an agreement reflecting new conditions on their behavior toward each other. Built into the contract was a three-month review of what was and was not working. Three years have elapsed since the mediation, and although they are not good friends, they have successfully worked together on committee assignments and have demonstrated capacities of empathy, listening, and problem solving with each other.

We use this case to encourage administrators, with caution of course, to consider ways to constructively use position power in interventions. This example highlights the unique window of opportunity available to most new leaders. Their staff want to demonstrate a willingness to work with a new leader, even if it requires some change. Similarly, staff not directly part of the conflict but affected by it are likely to support the change and work informally to help the parties sustain their changes.

ALTERNATIVES TO TRADITIONAL INTERVENTION STRATEGIES

Third party intervention practices are important skills to learn as part of a conflict resolution toolkit. Administrators need to develop special sensitivity to both the nuances and the obvious cultural differences of those we serve. We need to be sensitive to the complexities of ethics, power, values, and social justice. Usually parties in conflict operate with a great deal of pain. Our capacity to help them move beyond their pain, and beyond their positions, to find creative solutions is both satisfying and likely to increase the morale, effectiveness, and performance of all members of the department.

Facilitation and negotiation—two skills most often used by academic administrators to resolve conflicts—can be supplemented with other strategies. Informal third parties may have a continuing relationship with those in conflict but are not a primary party to the conflict. Nearly every department has someone who serves as an *informal peacemaker*. Behind closed doors, or over lunch, these people can diffuse hostilities, provide platforms for venting, and allow parties to consider options while "saving face." Based on the research of Deborah Kolb and her colleagues, we know that these peacemakers usually perform at least four important types of interventions: *supporting* as people complain, *reframing* to help parties better understand the situation, *translating* the perspectives of the other, and *orchestrating* opportunities for the parties in conflict to get resolution. These peacemaking colleagues may have little professional training but are clearly useful. When they intervene they are taking control and offering to be helpful, fair, effective, and even efficient. Administrators need to support and encourage people to engage in these activities. Some of the best conflict prevention is handled at this level.

Colleges and universities can give additional support to academic administrators when conflict seems out of control: ombuds programs, psychological services, human resources, grievance procedures, legal counsel, and disability leaves, to name a few. Professionals in each of these offices can offer precious counsel and referral based on your analysis of the conflict. In other words, you are not responsible for solving all conflicts within your unit. What we hope you can do, though, is better analyze the situation so that you can determine what to do, including whether or not you need to seek additional help.

If your college has an ombuds office, you need to determine the scope of their services. They essentially serve as informal data collectors, negotiators, mediators, facilitators, and counselors. They listen, provide suggestions, offer recommendations, and usually seek social justice for all parties. Some serve as neutrals; others serve as advocates. Almost always, they are independent and report either to the president or vice president of the college. Most ombuds are unusually skilled at interpersonal communication: listening, paraphrasing, reframing, and formulating suggestions. They are excellent shadow consultants to help you think through strategies as to how you might proceed.

Grievance policies and procedures also exist on nearly every campus. These policies articulate the types of conflicts that can be subjected to grievance processes. Most begin with an informal process of meeting with the parties involved. If the conflict cannot be resolved informally, there is a formal hearing, usually by an ad hoc group ready to serve when called. They listen carefully, ask questions, deliberate, and then make recommendations as to an appropriate resolution. It is essential that you are familiar with the processes available on your campus, as this is one more intervention strategy available to you.

Human resource management offices are another excellent resource. They provide consultation and direct intervention for problems between and among staff. Human resource offices exist to attract and provide continued support for a viable work force. If, in your analysis, you think the conflict has to do with individual job satisfaction, job involvement, commitment, absenteeism, turnover, or work performance, we encourage you to seek their counsel as this is their area of expertise.

Nearly all campuses have some sort of psychological services available to employees. Short-term counseling and referral assistance can be offered. When members of your staff are encountering significant life transitions—divorce, death of a loved one, illness, and so on—or abusing substances, you are likely to see changes in their behavior. Counseling departments can help you with ways to make referrals and provide support.

When conflicts get especially complicated and escalated, you may also want to seek legal counsel. The first step in the process is to discuss the situation with the person to whom you report. Even if legal recourse is unnecessary, it is helpful to know where you might be vulnerable. Other support offices such as equal employment opportunities and disability can give you specialized consultation around specific conflict situations.

SUMMARY

We have introduced a framework that builds upon the three levels of conflict analysis covered in Chapter Two. A careful conflict analysis needs to precede any consideration of its resolution. As an academic administrator you can and should use your position and relationships to intervene. And in addition to the four traditional intervention methods discussed—facilitation, negotiation, mediation, arbitration, and their hybrids—you also have available personnel from other departments across the college: ombuds, human resources, counseling, and legal.

We hope you realize that you need not resolve all conflicts in your department. Though you can and should develop special skills in preventing, defusing, and managing conflict, some situations are beyond your responsibilities or skills. At those times we encourage you to seek outside professional help.

8

Collaborating with Other Departments to Manage Conflict

CONFLICTS IN HIGHER education are ongoing. They can be psychologically draining, raise anxiety, lower morale, cause disengagement from others, and cause dissatisfaction with work and the college. If handled well, conflicts generate creative tension that can energize individuals, increase understanding of a problem, and improve empathy for the core values of colleagues. Conflict serves as a catalyst for growth and change. Conflict managed effectively can result in a comprehensive solution to the difficulty, improve and strengthen relationships with colleagues, and contribute to the professional development of those who learn from the experience.

Several examples of conflict—all cases with which we have worked—and how they might be handled have been used throughout this book. Because this book is targeted to the nonacademic side of higher education, we interviewed supervisors and department heads in universities. They told us that a great deal of conflict occurred between leaders of different departments and also with the academic staff members (faculty, chairs, and deans). Because the problems went beyond their areas of control, it was more difficult to manage them. Two examples follow that demonstrate how problems can be resolved more effectively when people from different departments work together, each adding a piece of information or a perspective on the problem that others do not have. The second case in this chapter provides an opportunity for you to analyze and generate solutions to another real conflict situation. We offer questions you might use as guidelines for your analysis. Some suggestions of our own for resolution will follow the final case.

DEPARTMENTS WORKING EFFECTIVELY TOGETHER

The following case is an example of how potentially serious problems can be managed when academic administrators on the support side of the university form close alliances with faculty. When collaboration replaces competition, problems within the university can be solved more easily. This case also illustrates the need for all individuals within higher education to be sensitive to the changing nature of the student body, to be available to help them, and to recognize that students are sometimes ill-equipped to solve problems that they created, not out of vindictiveness, but because they did not or could not anticipate the consequences of their acts and the impact they might have on others.

Jamal is a six-foot seven-inch first-generation college student who, although well-meaning and wanting very much to be liked, lacks some of the social skills that many of us take for granted. For example, he has run into problems with the Safety and Security Department, and one of the security guards has forbidden him to take his car on campus.

An example of his lack of social skills occurred in a class in which managing conflict was being discussed. In the middle of the lecture, he got up, walked through the light from the projector being used by the professor, left the room, went across the hall to the coffee shop, and came back in five minutes with a large bag of potato chips and a large cup of hot vegetable soup, once more walking through the stream of light. The students were sitting in a U-shaped configuration, and a student across the room motioned for him to share his potato chips. Jamal, again walking through the light from the projector, opened his bag of chips, making considerable noise in the process, and offered some to the other student. At this point an individual sitting next to that student also asked for some chips, which Jamal gave him, again with much noisy crinkling of cellophane. As Jamal walked one more time through the light from the projector, Dr. Benson said, "Jamal, you're 'dissing' me." Jamal, apparently upset, asked, "What'd I do? What'd I do?" Dr. Benson told him he was disrupting the class. Now obviously distressed, Jamal apologized, "Sorry, I didn't mean it."

Somewhat shaken, Jamal settled back in his chair and started removing the lid from the container of soup. The lid came off suddenly, and half the contents of the cup spilled on the floor. "Oh, I'm sorry. I'll get a paper towel from the men's room and wipe it up." Off he went and came back quickly. He got down on his hands and knees and began wiping up the spill. Unfortunately, the dry towels left a sticky mess on the floor, so when Jamal sat back down, each time he lifted his size fourteen running shoes, the soles of the shoes made a noise like Velcro being pulled apart. At the end of class he apologized to Dr. Benson profusely. His apology was accepted with good grace.

Two days later when class was in session again, Jamal was absent. Five minutes before class was over, Michael, a friend of his, knocked on the classroom door, looked through the window, and beckoned to Dr. Benson. When Dr. Benson opened the door, Michael said, "Jamal is in jail. I told him what you said in class to say when a friend is in trouble, 'Take it easy. It's not worth it,' but he didn't stop." Jamal had driven a female student who had broken her leg right up to the door of her classroom building, parked his car where it shouldn't have been, and helped her up the steps. Meanwhile, the security guard who had previously told Jamal he was forbidden to drive on campus at all, saw Jamal's car, drove up, and blocked it so he couldn't leave. Whoever started this new altercation is not clear, but fists began flying between Jamal and the security guard. The guard arrested Jamal, confiscated his car, and drove him off to jail, charging him with assault and battery.

Michael wanted to call Jamal's parents to explain what had happened before Jamal called them from jail, upset and excited. Since class was almost over, Dr. Benson dismissed the students and walked down the hall with Michael so he could use her office phone. On the way she saw that the Campus Council was in session in the conference room. Recognizing

Ed Barkley, the dean of students, as one of the participants, she motioned him to come to the door. She explained the situation and asked for his advice. Ed said that he would talk to José Cortes, a Safety and Security supervisor who fortunately was present at the meeting. Ed and Jose went to the local jail. The charges against Jamal were dropped and he was let go. Later, Ed telephoned Dr. Benson to tell her what had happened. He also called Jamal's parents to explain the misunderstanding to them. Later, the dean of students, the chief of safety and security, a psychologist from the Student Counseling Service, and Jamal had a meeting in which the incident and what lead up to it were discussed and resolved.

In this case, several departments—the dean of student affairs, chief of safety and security, director of the Student Counseling Service, and a faculty member—all worked together to resolve a problem. Jamal agreed to enter an anger management program run by the Student Counseling Service. His parents were satisfied with the manner in which the conflict was handled. The officer from Safety and Security also enrolled in an anger management course for staff. Without this kind of collaboration, a student might have been suspended from the university, his parents would be upset, and the member of the Safety and Security Department might have taken a highhanded approach with other students.

HOW STAFF TURNED A CAMPUS INTO A STUDENT-FRIENDLY COMMUNITY

A second case illustrates the need for the department heads of support staff to be included in the overall goals for the university. Students were leaving Cornwall University in large numbers, long before graduation. Dr. Anderson, the interim provost, had worked for an entire academic year persuading deans, department chairs, and faculty to devote more of their time to students. Faculty were now involving undergraduate students in their research, spending more time advising students about careers in their majors, taking them to national disciplinary conferences, and working as mentors to them. Because he had visited and heard about campus friendly colleges in which the support staff had also played a major role, Dr. Anderson wanted to involve the nonacademic support staff at his university.

He decided to turn the current problem over to his assistant, Dr. Tom Stewart, a highly regarded individual who had served on the faculty for more than thirty-five years. Tom was responsible, an excellent teacher, well liked by staff as well as students and faculty, and had a superb track record as a university citizen, contributing heavily in the area of university-wide service.

Tom decided to begin by investigating what students liked and disliked about the campus. Although the retention rate had increased this past year after all of the changes that had been made in the relationship between students and faculty, still a large number of students were leaving the university. Therefore, he decided to hold a series of focus groups for undergraduate students to look at their chief complaints and recommendations for changes in the university. The outcome of these groups unearthed the following recommendations from students:

Although a new large TV monitor had been installed in the Student Union Building, that room was always locked over the weekends. Students wanted access on Saturdays and Sundays. They also wanted access on weekends to rooms in the new fitness center, which had been closed to students who were not part of the athletic teams. However, Tom knew that maintenance staff did not want to exchange their weekday work for coverage on weekends.

Although the university owned a bus that was used for athletic events away from campus, it was generally not used on Sundays. Students wanted a series of trips planned, such as to Broadway shows, museums, other cultural events off-campus, as well as increasing events on campus. They wanted free transportation, and they would pay for tickets or admission to events.

Students wanted help in increasing attendance at athletic competitions. They suggested serving free or low cost food at such events.

Students wanted scrolling event monitors throughout campus so they could be more aware of events taking place on campus.

Students also requested better lighting on campus, immediate replacement of light bulbs on stairwells (the need for which maintenance staff were not aware), and implementation of a safety patrol who would monitor all sections of campus beginning at dusk and go on throughout the night.

They requested that they be treated with respect by all staff on campus, including security, enrollment management, and financial aid. Students felt that they had to wait too long in lines to register for classes, that classes they needed were sometimes closed, and that enrollment management staff did not treat them with respect. They also reported that security treated them "like mechanical objects."

Additional recommendations were the installation of new working clocks in all classrooms, more benches and tables throughout the campus, and improved signage on university grounds. Tom decided to add to this list providing free coffee in the café before and after evening classes.

When this information was shared with the provost, he was able to persuade a donor to give money for the student recommendations not covered by the budget. Since then the provost has kept students, staff, and faculty informed about progress on each of these requests. On the positive side, students feel that that provost is listening to them, and they can also observe that some of the changes they have requested are being carried out.

Tom has had a meeting with people who were the main obstacles to accomplishing some of these recommendations. Because he had once asked the Maintenance Department to cover weekend shifts and met with strong resistance, Tom Little, the dean of students, assumed that the directors of the Maintenance Department and the Safety and Security Department would object to having to provide weekend coverage for some of these requests without any additional compensation. Therefore, Tom assumed that they would refuse again. However, he was assured by Dr. Anderson that his request would be backed up by the provost's office.

Now let us see how this case relates to situations that might arise at your college or university.

- If you are an academic leader of student activities, library services, public safety, dining facilities, enrollment management, financial aid, residence halls, placement, the learning center, the advisement center, athletics, or admissions (if we have left out your particular area please add it), what can you do to motivate your staff to find ways of improving their relationships with students so they can also contribute to increasing student retention?

- How can you persuade staff supervisors that they need to provide weekend and evening coverage even though they will not be paid additional money to switch their shifts?

- Suppose that staff in your department tell you they are already doing their best when they interact with students. How do you handle this?

Conflict Diagnosis

By now you should have some sense of the multidimensional nature of many university problems. Some suggestions follow for your analysis of this conflict. As you may recall from the framework we introduced in Chapter Two (Figure 2.1, page 14), we will consider the micro levels (types, sources, dynamics), contextual levels (situations and identities), and macro levels (culture, traditions and structures) to fully understand the problem. What stands out as most pertinent?

Level I Analysis: Types, Sources, and Dynamics

With regard to the type of conflict, we consider the issues, hopes, orientation toward conflict, and levels of interaction. What *issues* have emerged? A few become obvious:

- Student retention at Cornwall is a significant problem. With lower enrollment, there is likely to be a budgetary impact university-wide.

- Staff do not perceive that their behavior has any impact on student retention. Therefore, they do not believe such additional work is part of their responsibilities, and they don't want to substitute working weekends for their regular hours.

- Dr. Anderson is an interim provost and, though he does not have as much power as he would if he were permanent in the position, he is initiating a new strategy for retention that will impact all departments.

What are the *hopes, aspirations, and goals* that have emerged? We can identify at least three:

- The administration represented by Drs. Anderson and Stewart wants to intervene on the significant problem of low student retention.

- The staff do not want to increase their workload.

- The student retention is down because students are not satisfied with the university.

Do we have any insight as to the *parties' orientation toward conflict?*

- Some supervisors probably hope the problem will go away if they don't respond to Tom's request. Therefore, they may be using an avoidance tactic.

- Some staff may actively challenge the program by using their power, threatening to file a grievance, or demanding extra pay. This may be an aggressive tactic.

Do we have any information about the *sources* of the conflict: the parties' relationships, needs, interests, values, and ideologies?

- The primary source of the conflict appears to be interest-based as students report having different needs—availability of increased weekend activities and improved safety measures—than the needs Tom assumed of the support staff. He expected to meet strong resistance from staff to having to provide weekend coverage without additional compensation.

- Another source of conflict appears to be relationship-based as students feel security treats them "like mechanical objects," registration makes them wait in long lines, and enrollment management does not respect them.

- If explored, we may find that the parties have some common interests, such as maintaining a high rate of retention.

Do we have any evidence of the *dynamics* of the conflict? Since overt conflict has not yet presented itself, the dynamics are still in a latent phase. However, when there are real and significant differences in *interests, power, perceived injustices,* and *needs,* the situation is ripe for conflict to erupt. These differences did emerge from Tom's investigation into what students liked and disliked about the campus. Tom was wise to conduct such an investigation and was fortunate to get funding to implement many of the student requests. Students felt listened to and changes were beginning to be made. These kinds of activities stave off conflict.

Level II Analysis: Situations and Identities

Considering the contextual issues of our conflict, are there situational and identity issues that are likely to be important and relevant?

- Dr. Anderson, interim provost, has made considerable progress over the year to increase the student retention rate. He was able to persuade deans, department chairs, and faculty to devote more time to students.

- Tom Stewart is a highly respected and well-liked member of the university community. Dr. Anderson leveraged Tom's talent and popularity to involve the nonacademic support staff in the problem of student retention.

- Tom's wisdom in conducting an investigation of student concerns is likely to have contributed to diminished resistance on the part of students. It also provided him with data to use when discussing changes with the staff.

Level III Analysis: Culture, Traditions, and Structures

Moving to the most macro level of analysis, we consider any factors related to the university's culture, traditions, and structures. What is apparent here? At least four stand out:

- The provost, though interim, introduced a significant change project. He worked an entire year persuading deans, chairs, and faculty to devote more time to students with the ultimate goal of improving student retention. This suggests that the interim nature of his work—position power—is less relevant at this university since there is evidence of competence. In other words, this provost is not a "lame duck" in this culture.

- Tom's investigation and movement to make changes based on student recommendations suggest that the student voice is important and highly regarded at this university.

- Tom's capacity to use collaborative problem solving is likely to be one of the reasons he is highly respected at the university. This is valued in the culture, and these kinds of skills are pertinent to interdepartmental conflicts. Tom's investigation and request for recommendations suggest that decisions get made based on input from multiple sources.

- There is also evidence that collaboration is preferred to aggressive tactics at this university. That is, Tom is meeting with the staff to try to make changes in student retention and implement student requests. He is not demanding these changes in an autocratic way (although he knows that he has support from the provost's office should he need it).

Intervention

Revisiting our framework introduced in Chapter Two, the final component of our analysis involves intervention. What would you do next? The traditional models of intervention include negotiation, facilitation, mediation, and arbitration. Are any of these appropriate to this situation? What prevention or intervention strategy would you suggest and why? We recommend the following:

Dr. Anderson is an interim provost. Given how serious the retention problem appeared to be, he did not believe he could wait until a new provost was selected to begin to fix the problem. He had already enlisted the support of the deans, department chairs, and faculty to increase their time and activities with students. Charging Tom Stewart, a highly regarded and experienced faculty member, to work on the problem gave the problem legitimacy and signaled to the community that this was a high priority. Tom's investigation demonstrated that he wanted to know what the issues were from the students' perspective—the primary stakeholder in student retention. Students gave him feedback with recommendations. The provost got funding for many of the recommendations. What remains is enlisting support on the part of the staff. This change is likely to impact their workload and work life.

One strategy Tom could use is a *facilitated dialogue* with staff. He could present the results of his investigation with students including their recommendations. He could demonstrate that Dr. Anderson had successfully obtained outside funding to pay for some of the changes. The goal of the meeting should be to request staff support for increased student retention and generate suggestions that could help implement the recommendations.

It is important that Tom present a perspective of "we're all in this together" instead of "the provost's office insists that staff make changes." The latter will only create an adversarial relationship between the staff and the students (and perhaps between the staff and the provost's office). Tom might ask staff to form a task force to consider the situation, create new staffing options, and propose low- or no-cost incentives for staff initially willing to make changes in their staffing patterns. This dialogue must take place in an atmosphere not of blame or accusation, but rather of "although you are doing a great job, what more can we do to create an environment that will make this campus a satisfying experience for students? What other ideas do you have that will help reduce the high drop-out rate of students?"

After Tom receives the recommendations from the staff, he may convene another meeting between student and staff representatives to address increased student retention and prepare a combined list of recommendations to be forwarded to the provost.

SUMMARY

We hope that this chapter has given you an opportunity to (1) look at the importance of having the nonacademic support staff and the academic part of the university work collaboratively so that each can contribute their perspectives, experience, knowledge, attitude, and skills to preventing and, if necessary, solving conflicts within the university; and (2) try your diagnostic and intervention skills on a case that exemplifies conflict resolution by all sides of an academic institution. If successful, you should have learned that the key to effective conflict intervention is an accurate analysis of the problem and anticipation of potential debilitating conflict. If you take sufficient time to fully understand the problem, not only can you develop strategies to fix it, but you can also learn new ways to prevent future conflict.

Academic administrators who are wise about conflict analysis and take risks with their interventions will model to their staff that this is a healthy and vibrant department in which to work. This will foster high morale and job satisfaction, which ultimately lead to good performance. It is our hope that with practice you will be able to take greater risks with increased confidence because of your thorough and thoughtful analysis of the conflict situation.

To create universities that manage conflict successfully, we will need one another. Therefore, we wish you success in turning conflicts into problems to be solved, competition into collaboration, and friction into improved relationships and ongoing professional development.

RECOMMENDED READING

Asch, S. *Social Psychology.* Englewood Cliffs, N.J.: Prentice-Hall, 1952.

Barsky, A. E. *Conflict Resolution for the Helping Professions.* Belmont, Calif.: Wadsworth: Brooks/Cole Social Work, 2000.

Beck, A. T. *Cognitive Therapy and the Emotional Disorders.* New York: International Universities Press, 1976.

Bridges, W. *Transitions: Making Sense of Life's Changes.* Cambridge, Mass.: Perseus Books, 1980.

Cheldelin, S. I., Druckman, D., and Fast, L., *Conflict: From Analysis to Intervention.* London and New York: Continuum, 2003.

Cloke, K. *Mediating Dangerously: The Frontiers of Conflict Resolution.* San Francisco: Jossey-Bass, 2001.

Cloke, K., and Goldsmith, J. *Resolving Conflicts and Work: A Complete Guide for Everyone on the Job.* San Francisco: Jossey-Bass, 2000.

Coombs, C. H. "The Structure of Conflict." *American Psychologist,* 1987, *42,* 355–363.

Dutsch, M., and Coleman, P. T. (eds.). *Handbook of Conflict Resolution: Theory and Practice.* San Francisco: Jossey-Bass, 2000.

Fisher, R., Ury, W., and Patton, B. *Getting to Yes: Negotiating Agreement Without Giving In* (3rd ed.). New York: Penguin, 1997.

Folger, J. P., Poole, M. S., and Stutman, R. K. *Working Through Conflict: Strategies for Relationships, Groups, and Organizations* (3rd ed.). New York: Longman, 1997.

Holton, Susan A. (ed.). *Mending the Cracks in the Ivory Tower: Strategies for Conflict Management in Higher Education.* Bolton, Mass.: Anker, 1998.

Kolb, D. M., and Associates. *When Talk Works: Profiles of Mediators.* San Francisco: Jossey-Bass, 1994.

Lewin, K. *Field Theory in Social Science: Selected Theoretical Papers.* New York: Harper and Row, 1951.

Lucas, A. F. *Strengthening Departmental Leadership: A Team-Building Guide for Chairs in Colleges and Universities.* San Francisco: Jossey-Bass, 1996.

Lucas, A. F., and Associates. *Leading Academic Change: Essential Roles for Department Chairs.* San Francisco: Jossey-Bass, 2000.

Mayer, B. *The Dynamics of Conflict Resolution: A Practitioner's Guide.* San Francisco: Jossey-Bass, 2000.

Pondy, L. R. "Organizational Conflict: Concepts and Models." *Administrative Science Quarterly,* 1967, *12,* 296–320.

Rice, R. E., and Sorcinelli, M. D. "Can the Tenure Process Be Improved?" In R. P. Chait (ed.), *The Question of Tenure.* Cambridge, Mass.: Harvard Press, 2002.

Schachter, S., and Gazzaniga, M. (eds.). *Extending Psychological Frontiers: Selected Works of Leon Festinger.* New York: Russell Sage Foundation, 1989.

Schrock-Shenk, C. (ed.). *Mediation and Facilitation Training Manual: Foundations and Skills for Constructive Conflict Transformation* (4th ed.). Akron, Penn.: Mennonite Conciliation Service, 2000.

Schwarz, R. M. *The Skilled Facilitator: Practical Wisdom for Developing Effective Groups.* San Francisco: Jossey-Bass, 1994.

Seligman, M.E.P. *Learned Optimism.* New York: Knopf, 1991.

Seligman, M.E.P. *What You Can Change—and What You Can't: The Complete Guide to Successful Self Improvement.* New York: Fawcett Columbine, 1995.

Seligman, M.E.P. *Authentic Happiness: Using the New Positive Psychology to Realize Your Potential for Lasting Fulfillment.* New York: Free Press, 2002.

Sherif, M. *In Common Predicament: Social Psychology of Intergroup Conflict and Cooperation.* Boston: Houghton Mifflin, 1966.

Thomas, K. W., and Kilmann, R. H. *Thomas-Kilmann Conflict Mode Instrument.* XICOM, Inc. 1974.

Thomas, W. "Conflict and Conflict Management." In M. D. Dunnette (ed.), *Handbook of Industrial and Organizational Psychology.* New York: Rand McNally, 1976.

Tuchman, B. W. "Developmental Sequences in Small Groups." *Psychological Bulletin,* 1965, *63,* 384–399.

Warters, W. C. *Mediation in the Campus Community: Designing and Managing Effective Programs.* San Francisco: Jossey-Bass, 1999.

Wilmot, W. W., and Hocker, J. L. *Interpersonal Conflict* (5th ed.). Boston: McGraw-Hill, 1998.

INDEX

A

Academic administrator: collaborative problem solving of, 94–96; conflicting and ambiguous roles of, 26–27; and group formation, 55–56; as intervener, 79; as team leader, 50–51; position power of, 5, 83–84; and role overload, 27

Accommodation, as reaction to conflict, 15, 52

Active listening, in conflict management, 5, 28, 43, 46, 48, 54, 63–64

Affirmation, in conflict resolution, 43

Aggression, as reaction to conflict, 15

Anger management, 43

Appreciative inquiry, in facilitation, 81–82

Arbitration: in collective bargaining, 87, 88; combined with mediation (med-arb), 88; defined, 22; impartial third parties in, 88

Asch, S., 69

Assisted negotiation. *See* Facilitation

Authentic communication, 7

Avoidance, as reaction to conflict, 15, 43–44, 51–52, 56

B

Beck, A., 28

Bridges, W., 10

Budgeting decisions, and intergroup conflict, 5–6, 68

C

Categorization: derogatory and inappropriate, 5–6, 76; and intergroup conflict, 74; and group differentiation, 72–73

Change: as precursor to conflict, 8–10; stress and, 10; transitional nature of, 10–11

Class-based conflicts, 17

Collaboration, as reaction to conflict, 15, 53–54

Collegial culture, 19–20

Competition: and intergroup conflict, 68, 70; and interunit threats, 4–5; for scarce resources, 3, 4, 9

Complaints, creating space for, 7–8

Compromise, as reaction to conflict, 15

Conflict: administrator-faculty, 5; common precursors to, 8; and competition for scarce resources, 4, 68; constructive, 7–8, 57, 93; defined, 1; destructive, 3–7; dynamics, 16–17; and higher education's organizational context, 3; identity issues in, 17–18, 67–68, 72–74; and learned coping skills, 2–3; orientations to, 15; and perceived differences/injustices, 16–17; personalized, 45; situational and social contexts of, 18; sources and types of, 15–16

Conflict analysis framework, 13–23, 14*fig*, 75, 77–78, 79*fig*

Conflict diagnosis, 99–103; and choice of intervention, 102–103; conflict dynamics and, 15–17; identity and situation issues in, 17–18, 75; institutional culture and traditions in, 19–21; social and psychological dimensions of, 15–17; sources of conflict and, 16; types of conflict and, 15–16

Conflict escalation: common results of, 6; conditions for, 4–6; harmful effects of, 43–44; threatening influence patterns in, 5

Conflict prevention strategies, 58–61

Conflict resolution skills, 42–45. *See also* Problem solving

Coombs, C. H., 39

Criticism, in conflict resolution, 43–44

Cultural values, and conflict resolution, 76

Culture, institutional: collegial versus managerial, 19–20; and departmental norms, 20, 49–51

D

Departmental groups, developmental stages of, 54–57

Difficult people, strategies for dealing with, 28, 58–59, 84–85

Diversity training, 76

Druckman, D., 13

E

Economy: and competition for scarce resources, 3, 4, 9, 68; market versus prestige, 20

Employee performance inadequacy, supervisor's approach to, 59–60

Empowerment, and transformation-based negotiation, 86

F

Facilitated dialogue strategy, 103

Facilitation: choice of facilitator in, 47, 80; facilitator role in, 81; history of, 80; large-group, 82; versus mediation, 82; models, 81–82; process, 46–47, 81; supplements to, 90

Faculty-administrator relationship, 5, 94–96

Family responsibilities, and role conflict, 26, 84–85

Fast, L., 13

G

Gestalt Institute of Cleveland, 80

Grievance policies, 91

Griping sessions, 7

Group identity, and intergroup conflict, 67–68, 72–74

Group meetings: "stop action" strategy in, 61–62; task and relationship responsibilities in, 62–64

Group(s): developmental stages of, 54–57; facilitation, practice of, 80; social influence of, 69–70

H

Higher education, organizational context for conflict in, 3

Hocker, J., 1

Human resource office, 91

I

Intergroup conflict, 67–76; belligerent influence patterns in, 4–5, 70, 73–74; categorization and polarization in, 70, 72–74, 76; and competition for limited resources, 5–6, 68, 70; conformity and compliance in, 69–72; escalation of, 68, 71–72; historical roots of, 68; influence of group identity in, 67–68, 72–74; and intergroup interaction, 74; interventions, 74–75, 82

Interpersonal conflict, 37–48, 67; basic outcomes of, 38; causes of, 39–40; interventions, 41–42, 45–48; and need to save face, 47–48; personalization of, 45; stages of, 40–42

Interventions, 77–92; alternative, 90–92; choice of, 77–78; empowerment and recognition in, 86; and grievance processes, 91; hybrid, 88–89; for identity-based conflicts, 18; and through ombuds office, 91; by peacemaking colleagues, 90; power–based, 83–84, 89; social context of, 18;

structural, 21, 75; third party involvement in, 22, 42, 46, 87, 88; types of, 21–22, 79, 80*fig*

Intragroup conflict, 49–66, 67; and departmental norms, 50–51; diversity and, 58; dysfunctional behavior in, 56, 57; facilitation as intervention for, 82; and group development stages, 54–57; strategies for handling and preventing, 51–54, 58–65; team approach to, 53–54

Intrapersonal conflict, 25–36; and conflicting obligations, 26; impact of stress on, 27; and negative thinking, 27–35

K

Kolb, D., 90

L

Legal counsel, 92

Legal system: arbitration and, 88; and rights-based negotiation, 85–86

Lewin, K., 80

M

Managerial culture, 19–20

Mediation: combined with arbitration (med-arb), 88; defined, 22; versus facilitation, 82; historical use of, 87; mediator's role in, 87; usefulness and practical outcomes of, 87–88

Meeting audit, 61

Mentoring, 58

N

National Training Laboratories, 80

Negative thinking, 27–35; characteristics and effects of, 28–29; and cognitive restructuring, 29–32; and fundamental attribution error, 33–34; and negative reinforcement, 30; and self-serving bias, 34–35; supervisor's handling of, 28, 32–33, 58–59

Negotiation: interest–based, 84–85; in intragroup conflict, 43; power-based, 83–84; process, 21; relationship between process and outcome in, 82–83; rights-based, 85–86; supplements to, 90; transformation-based, 86

Nonjudgmental listening. *See* Active listening

O

Ombuds program interventions, 42, 46, 91

P

Personal characteristics, attacks on, 5–6

Pondy, L. R., 40

Power: as basis of negotiation, 83–84; careful use of, 5; in conflict management, 52–53, 56, 83–84

Prestige economy, and collegial culture, 20

Problem solving: defining and reframing conflict in, 46; in facilitation, 81–82; paraphrasing and active listening in, 43, 48, 63–64; steps in, 45–48

Procrastination, and negative thinking, 29–30

Psychological services, on-campus, 91

R

Relationship-based conflict, 16

Rice, E., 19

S

Schachter, S., 69

Search and screen committees, confidentiality in, 62–63

Self-talk, negative versus constructive, 29–30

Seligman, M.E.P., 28

Sherif, M., 69

Situational factors, in conflict analysis, 18, 75

Sorcinelli, M. D., 19
Stress: physiological signs of, 41, 45, 49; and role overload, 27; significant change and, 10
Structures, academic, 20–21
Structural interventions, 21, 75
Supervisory role: ambiguity and conflict in, 26–27; of evaluation versus mentoring, 26; and negative thinking, 28, 32–33, 58–59
Supervisory support network, 44
Support staff-student conflict, case study of, 96–103

T

Task forces, 75
Tavistock Institute of Human Relations, 80

Third parties: neutrality of, 79; role of, 22, 42, 46, 87, 88
Thomas, K. W., 51
Threatening influence patterns: and conflict development/escalation, 4–5; and intergroup conflict, 70, 73–74
Traditions, and institutional change, 20
Transitions: as source of conflict, 8–10; stages of, 11
Tuchman, B. W., 55

W

Wilmot, W., 1